GLENN RAWSON STORIES

FEATURING THE ARTWORK OF KELSY AND JESSE LIGHTWEAVE

New Testament Stories

Glenn Rawson

© 2023 Glenn J. Rawson

Thank you to everyone at the Glenn Rawson Stories team that helped make this book possible: Jean, Kristen, Dianna, Julie, Sara, Jason, June, Wilmie, and Manny. We would like to thank the team at Seagull Printing for their superior printing quality. Without the help of these amazing people, we would not be able to share share inspirational stories in the capacity.

All Rights Reserved. No part of this book may be reproduced in any form or by any means without permission from the authors. Requests for permission may be made by contacting the authors at GlennRawsonStories.com. The views expressed herein are the responsibility of the author.

Artwork provided by the creators at www.lightweave.me

ISBN 979-8-88526-325-2

Printed in the United States of America

Other Inspirational Titles By Glenn

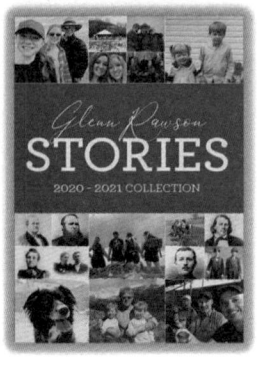 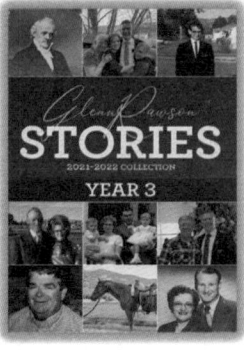 

Get These Great Titles At
GlennRawsonStories.com

Customer Submitted Book Reviews

"Thank you for your stories and love of history."

- Grace C.

"Absolutely brilliant and inspiring. The stories just keep getting better."

-Ron H.

"I have enjoyed all the books I have received from you. I am especially happy with Stories of the Hymns. You were correct when you said that we wouldn't think of the songs in the same way. Thank you!

- Gloria C.

Subscribe to Glenn's Stories at
GlennRawsonStories.com

Table Of Contents

Prologue X
Artist Feature..XII

1. The Annunciation.. 1
2. The Birth 4
3. Why the Angels Sang 7
4. Bethlehem and John the Baptist 9
5. Joseph the Carpenter..11
6. The Witness of the Shepherds 13
7. The Wise men 16
8. Herod the Great.. 19
9. Bethlehem Today 22
10. The Prophecy of Simeon 25
11. The Boy Jesus 28
12. Temptation 30
13. Friends Helping Friends 33
14. Water Into Wine 35
15. Come to Jesus 37
16. Photina the Samaritan Woman 39
17. The Nobleman's Son 41
18. Jesus Visits Nazareth.. 43
19. The Power of His Word....................................... 45
20. The Palsied Man and His Friends 47
21. The Paradox of Joy 49
22. The Withered Hand 52
23. Skeptics and the Faithful.................................... 54

24. THE WIDOW OF NAIN 57
25. THE WEEPING WOMAN 59
26. IN THE BOAT WITH US 61
27. JAIRUS 63
28. CLOSE ENOUGH TO TOUCH 65
29. FAITH TO WALK ON WATER 67
30. THE DAY IN GENNESARET 69
31. THE BREAD OF LIFE 71
32. THE GENTILE WOMAN 73
33. THEY WERE OFFENDED 75
34. THE DEAF MAN BY GALILEE 77
35. UPON THIS ROCK 79
36. LORD, I BELIEVE 82
37. THE CHASTENING OF THE LORD 84
38. CLOTHED WITH GLORY 87
39. PATIENCE 89
40. THE MASTER TEACHER 91
41. THE ADULTEROUS WOMAN 93
42. THE MAN BORN BLIND 96
43. MARTHA AND MARY 99
44. THE GOOD SAMARITAN 101
45. THE PRODIGAL'S HOPE 104
46. LESSONS FROM LAZARUS 106
47. THAT ONE LEPER 109
48. THE IMPORTUNATE WIDOW 111
49. OBEDIENCE ALWAYS 113

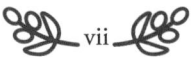

50. The Pharisee and the Publican 115
51. Bartimaeus 117
52. Mary's Kindness 120
53. The Cleansing 122
54. Hypocrities... 124
55. The Widows Mite 127
56. Happy Are Ye 129
57. Be of Good Cheer... 131
58. The Annunciation 133
59. Love As Jesus Expressed It 135
60. Gethsemane 138
61. Turn to Pray 141
62. The Body and Blood 143
63. Pain...145
64. Pontius Pilate... 147
65. Watch the Lamb..149
66. Thing of Naught 152
67. Serve Thy Mother..154
68. Jesus the Pioneer...156
69. Resurrection Morning...158
70. The Saints Who Arose 160
71. The Stranger on the Road 162
72. Lovest Thou Me 165
73. Change... 168
74. Saul..170
75. Cornelius and Peter...172
About the Author..175
About the Artist 177

PROLOGUE - GLENN RAWSON

PROLOGUE

I am a Christian. I love the Lord, Jesus Christ, and I am striving each day to live like Him and follow Him. He is my Savior, Redeemer, and friend. I have not always known or believed in Him, but that changed when I was a young college student. Since that time more than forty years ago, He has been my greatest subject of study. I have devoted more hours to learning what I could of Him than any other person or subject.

In the 1990's, I was invited to begin a weekly Sunday radio series where I would tell inspirational stories on the air. Over the ensuing years, the Lord was my most frequent subject, and the New Testament my favorite text.

This book is a collection of some of those stories. They are mostly the old familiar stories of the New Testament, told in my words, with insights gleaned over years of study and inspiration. I especially hope you will read them to children.

They represent the interpretation of one man. I alone am responsible for the interpretations shared here. I am indebted to a talented and skilled team who asked for this book and helped me get it ready for you.

In order that you might understand the layout of the book, it flows chronologically through the life of the Savior—from the Christmas story to the Resurrection, and beyond. The location where each story took place is noted at the top of the story and a general notation of the chapters of scripture is at the bottom.

Even after decades of study and worship, I still feel inadequate to speak of Him and use His name. I am just a lowly disciple of the Master, but I offer this book in hopes that someone, somewhere, will be brought a little closer to Him.

Glenn Rawson

Call Of The Master

And I will give thee the treasures of darkness, and hidden riches of secret places, that thou mayest know that I, the Lord, which call thee by thy name, am the God of Israel.

Isaiah 45:3

When the call comes.... Will we be ready to seek the hidden riches? Realizing that we all have busy lives, we often find it hard to see beyond the tasks at hand. We can become so busy that tasks start to become perfunctory in nature. In the midst of the tumult, it frequently comes when least expected–the call to do something greater. The hope of this symbolic art piece is to remind us of time, work, and the purpose of our earthly experience. Hopefully, we can make time to calm the waters surrounding our busy endeavors, reflect upon existence, and perhaps see the Savior, standing along the shore, ready to issue His call.

- Kelsy and Jesse Lightweave

No Greater Love

The Eternal Ruler of the Universe, our God and Creator, King and Ruler of all, is all-knowing and all-powerful. Of all the titles and all the names of praise available, He has asked us to call him "Father." The simple relationship between a loving, caring father and his child is all we need to understand in order to know how He feels about each one of us.

Kelsy and Jesse Lightweave

Return

Return is a symbolic piece that depicts the account of Luke 17:11-19, when the 10th leper returned to the Savior to bring him praise—ready for further light and knowledge. The Savior then sent him on his way, commending his act of faith in him. This piece contains symbolic elements to depict our relationship with our Savior. The hope is to help ground the viewer's roots in the foundation the Lord has created for us, feasting upon his living water, and reaching to heaven, the source of light and everlasting life.

"And he took bread, and gave thanks, and brake it, and gave unto them, saying, This is my body which is given for you: this do in remembrance of me." Luke 22:19 describes one of the final ministering acts of the Savior before he descended below all to bring forth the well of living water for all human kind. One of his last requests was that we remember.

Remembering constitutes more than just a thoughtful reflection of the Lord's deeds on this earth. It embodies living alongside the Savior and returning to the source of light consistently and faithfully. Luke 17 gives the symbolic account of the 10th leper who not only felt immense joy and love for the salvation from crippling physical captivity, but also exercised great faith in returning to his Maker in an unequivocal statement of remembrance.

His healing hand lifts us as we choose to remember our Maker and reflect Him in all our works and deeds. Let us return to Him, on humble knees, to learn of His will for us, that He may see our gratitude reflected in our souls. Let us be as a tree, ever fixed in the ground where the life-giving water the Savior procured for us resides, reaching unto heaven where the everlasting light heals and revitalizes our mortal bonds.

Our Creator and Sustainer will never hold back the water and light we need to be his instruments. He will build us higher and greater than we could ever think possible. Through faith in his word, even the smallest of seeds can become the greatest of trees. As we frequently turn to Him and reflect his work in our lives, He will build us, He will heal us, and he will send us forth saying, "Arise, go thy way: thy faith hath made thee whole" (Luke 17:19).

- Kelsy and Jesse Lightweave

The Annunciation

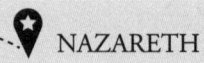 NAZARETH   *Scriptures: Luke 2*

As mortals, we have a tendency to resist change. Our Father in Heaven wisely prepares us before critical decisions need to be made. He does that oftentimes by schooling our feelings in advance, and informing our agency. In that light, would you please consider what happened to Mary on that day with Gabriel?

"And in the sixth month," Luke records, "the angel Gabriel was sent from God unto a city of Galilee, named Nazareth" (Luke 1:26).

He was sent, Luke continues, "To a virgin espoused to a man whose name was Joseph, of the house of David; and the virgin's name was Mary" (Luke 1:27).

By merciful providence, Mary was not to be alone through all that was ahead of her to bear God's son. Joseph, of kingly descent, was Mary's chosen companion, and as he would so often prove, he was her protector.

"And the angel came in unto her, and said, Hail thou that art highly favoured, the Lord is with thee: blessed art thou among women" (Luke 1:28).

Mary stands preeminent, chosen and blessed among women because of her faith. Even her name rightly means "exalted." Please note, to our Father in Heaven, she was precious.

"And when she saw him, she was troubled at his saying, and cast in her mind what manner of salutation this should be" (Luke 1:29).

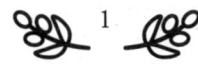

The Annunciation

The sight of the angel frightened Mary, and evidently confused her. Why was he greeting her in such a manner, and with such reverence?

Seeing this, the angel responded, "…Fear not, Mary: for thou hast found favour with God. And behold, thou shalt conceive in thy womb, and bring forth a son, and shalt call his name JESUS" (Luke 1:30-31).

As it is, motherhood is the highest, holiest calling on earth – but to be the mother of Jesus the Christ? I can't even imagine! Her son would be as He was named. The name "Jesus" means "Savior."

"He shall be great, and shall be called the Son of the Highest: and the Lord God shall give unto him the throne of his father David: And he shall reign over the house of Jacob forever; and of his kingdom there shall be no end" (Luke 1:32-33).

This promise to Mary must have strengthened her and stayed with her for the rest of her life. No matter the mortal realities, her son was a prince – the "Prince of Peace" – worlds without end. No son ever brought more honor and glory to his mother than did Jesus. But – to have a son, and not be married…?

"Then said Mary into the angel, How shall this be, seeing I know not a man?" (Luke 1:34).

As yet, Mary still did not understand or comprehend who, what, and how her son was to be.

In response, Gabriel said, "…The Holy Ghost shall come upon thee, and the power of the Highest shall overshadow thee: therefore also that holy thing which shall be born of thee shall be called the Son of God" (Luke 1:35).

This son was to be like no other before or after. He was the only son God ever sired into mortality, the only begotten in

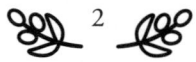

the flesh. The Son of God Himself was coming to earth, and she, Mary of Nazareth, was to prepare His physical tabernacle, and be His earthly mother.

And then, as if to confirm Mary's overwhelmed faith, Gabriel said, "And, behold, thy cousin Elisabeth, she hath also conceived a son in her old age: and this is the sixth month with her, who was called barren. For with God nothing shall be impossible" (Luke 1:36-37).

When all the powers of hell would be let loose on Mary and her family, she would always remember and know this truth: God can do the impossible. What serenity and peace this proven truth must have been to her later.

The call was now explained and extended. Mary's calling and election in mortality had now been offered to her. Now what would she do?

In meek submission Mary said, "…Behold, the handmaid of the Lord; be it unto me according to thy word…" (Luke 1:38).

I find it most notable that before Jesus would ever say in Gethsemane, "…not my will, but thine, be done," His mother would say it first. (Luke 22:42)

Besides her Almighty Son, was there ever a mortal who accepted so much responsibility with so few words? My soul overflows with reverence, awe, and love for Mary! Whatmanner of woman was she – is she, and how did Heaven look upon her? I can't even find the words!

2

THE BIRTH

BETHLEHEM — *Scriptures: Luke 2*

I want to tell a familiar story with this in mind: Christmas is all about love.

"And it came to pass in those days, that there went out a decree from Caesar Augustus, that all the world should be taxed " (Luke 2:1).

You know, as Caesar and the oppressive Roman Empire counted and taxed the goods of life from its subjects, ("And this taxing was first made when Cyrenius was governor of Syria", (Luke 2:2), at the same time, a true king was born who would also number His sheep, but would free them and give them the abundance of life – not take it.

Sometimes I wonder why that's in there. The book of Luke was a letter written to a friend. This parenthetical comment was directed by Luke to his friend Theophilus, to give him a point of time reference for the beginning of his story.

Another thought is that every year we send Christmas cards with expressions of love, faith, and greeting. So, what does that make the Book of Luke then? – the world's first Christmas card?

"And all went to be taxed, every one unto his own city. And Joseph also went up from Galilee, out of the city of Nazareth, into Judaea, unto the city of David, which is called Bethlehem; (because he was of the house and lineage of David:) To be taxed with Mary, his espoused wife, being great with child" (Luke 2:3-5).

No matter what the customs of the Jews, Joseph and Mary returned to Bethlehem because God wanted them to, because Jesus had to be born in Bethlehem to fulfill the words of the prophets. We can only imagine how arduous that journey must have been for Mary, who was almost ready to have the baby. Yet sacrifice, then and now, brings forth the blessings of heaven.

"And so it was, that, while they were there, the days were accomplished that she should be delivered. And she brought forth her firstborn son,…" (Luke 2:6-7).

Jesus was Mary's firstborn, and the birthright son of Joseph's family. Later, Mary would have at least four more sons and at least two daughters. So I guess you could say in more ways than one, Jesus stood at the head of a large family.

"… and wrapped him in swaddling clothes,…" (Luke 2:7).

To swaddle was to wrap the newborn to provide comfort and security. Isaiah prophesied in the Old Testament that a virgin would conceive and bring forth a son, and then he said right after that, that "…Butter and honey shall he eat…" (Isaiah 7:12-15), meaning the son of the virgin. Butter and honey were staples in the diet of the poor. The meaning seems to be that Jesus would be born in poverty.

"… and laid him in a manger; because there was no room for them in the inn[s]" (Luke 2:7).

Mary's condition would have been obvious. Imagine if an expectant mother came to your door. Could you ever turn her away? Yet in the hardness of their hearts, no one would make room for her in the inns.

Descended from the royal courts on high, the Prince of Peace, the King of Heaven, was born in His own city, among His own people, in a stable. Bethlehem marked the

The Birth

beginning of the journey for the Savior, who would descend below all things, that He might rise above all things.

My friends, I hope with all of my heart that the love of the Savior fills your heart this Christmas, and that love spreads to all men as you make room for Him.

Why the Angels Sang

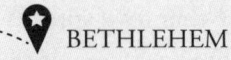 BETHLEHEM   *Scriptures: Luke 2*

On the night that Jesus was born, the Angel of the Lord announced His coming and told the shepherds how to find him.

"And suddenly there was with the angel a multitude of the heavenly host praising God, and saying, Glory to God in the highest and on earth peace, good will toward men" (Luke 2:13-14).

Can you imagine that holy night when an innumerable chorus of angels stood by in the heavens, so filled with joy and anticipation that they burst forth in songs of praise and adoration? Literally, heaven sang while earth slept. Now clearly, those angels understood something that the mortals beneath them did not. The angels not only knew what Jesus would be. They knew what He had been.

Jesus, or Jehovah, as He was known before He was born, was in the beginning with the Father. He was the firstborn of all our Father's children, and was His beloved and chosen from the very beginning. Indeed, He was greater than us all, even before He was born.

From the beginning, Jesus was that spiritual rock that led the children of God to salvation; and yet, He was as meek and lowly as a lamb. Indeed, from the very beginning, Jesus prepared himself to die as that sacrificial lamb, that we might live.

All men from Adam to Christ exercised faith and received the benefits of an atonement that would happen, just as we today exercise faith in the very one that did. Who can say why, but Jehovah came to this world to work out the infinite and eternal atonement.

The God of Heaven was coming here to take a mortal body. The God of Glory stripped himself of that glory and came to earth as a tiny babe to work out his salvation – and ours. The Savior and Redeemer was born that night in Bethlehem. The heavens understood who He was, and what He was, and what He would do – and they could not be restrained from singing.

Now I say to you: the more we know Him, the more we too, like the angels at His birth, will want to worship and sing in praise.

4

Bethlehem and John the Baptist

 SOMEWHERE IN JUDEA   *Scriptures: Luke 1*

Have you ever noticed how often we tell the story of Christmas and skip over the birth of John the Baptist? I don't think we should. To neglect John in telling that story is like neglecting your preparations for Christmas until the morning of.

Before there was John the Baptist, there was John the baby.

Before Matthew, Mark, Luke, and John wrote of Jesus, John the Baptist kept a record first. As in his life, John pointed people to Jesus, so too did he in his birth.

Before Gabriel came to Mary, he appeared to an old man named Zacharias in the Temple. "Fear not, Zacharias," he said, "thy prayer is heard; and thy wife Elizabeth shall bear thee a son, and thou shalt call his name John" (Luke 1:13). The angel promised that this little boy would bring much joy to many people, but not just because he was a baby, but because he would "be great in the sight of the Lord.... Many of the children of Israel shall he turn to the Lord their God" (Luke 1:15-16). John would go before the Savior and "... make ready a people prepared for the Lord" (Luke 1:17).

Zacharias struggled to believe what he was hearing. I don't blame him! Elizabeth was an older woman. Nonetheless, Mary's miraculous conception was not the first. Before Mary went into hiding with a child she could not explain, Elizabeth was there first.

One day, a beautiful young woman, sent by an angel, came into the courtyard of Elizabeth's home and called out a greeting. In the womb, John leaped for joy, and he and his mother were filled with the Holy Ghost. It is sublime that at that moment John bore witness of the Messiah before he even had a voice. The two sons of prophecy and their sainted mothers spent the next three months together.

As John prepared the way for Jesus, so Elizabeth prepared and consoled Mary. Before the people heard the shepherds' witness of a coming Messiah, they were astonished at the new voice and testimony of Zacharias.

His prophecies resonated through the hills and hearts of the Jews, filling them with grand expectations. Then and later, all who ever knew John could not wait to meet Jesus.

On the night of the Savior's birth in Bethlehem, John was three months old in Hebron. Knowing what Elizabeth knew of Mary and the bond they shared, I wonder how far away she really was from her young cousin.

When Herod's soldiers came, you know they were looking for two famous babies – not one.

While the angel sent Joseph and Mary into Egypt to save Jesus, Zacharias sent John and Elizabeth into the wilderness. Joseph and Jesus escaped, but the soldiers killed Zacharias. He would not give up his son. As Jesus grew up with his Father, hewing wood, so John grew up in the wilderness, eating locusts and wild honey without his father. As Jesus waited and prepared to bring men to His Father, so John waited and prepared to bring men to Jesus.

Luke's story of Christmas tells of a special babe whose birth pointed men to Jesus' birth and John was born to prepare the way for Him. God grant that we now be like John, that in all that we are, all that we say, all that we do, people want to learn of Christ.

Joseph the Carpenter

NAZARETH

As a baby, the Lord Jesus was as weak and vulnerable as any other child ever born. In the wisdom of God, a man was chosen as a protector of the Christ Child and His mother. That man was Joseph, the carpenter.

There's a principle that says, "Where much is given, much is required." Joseph was blessed with the love and the hand of the most beautiful maiden in all the land – Mary. She was a precious and chosen young woman. Joseph was also entrusted to protect her and shepherd the development of God's only Begotten Son. It was not a small trust. Please consider the following the next time you read the scriptures about Joseph.

Obedient to the angel, and contrary to his own mind, Joseph married Mary and named her child Jesus. What if Joseph had been an extremist and decided to have her stoned as an adulteress? Obedient to the law, Joseph returned to Bethlehem to be taxed with Mary, his wife, and thus he fulfilled the prophecy. What if he had refused, and the trip was never made?

Devotedly, upon arriving in Bethlehem, Joseph sought the best for Mary in the delivery of her child, going to numerous inns. But since no one would make room for them, at least he found a stable. Faithfully, Joseph brought Jesus and Mary to the temple to do for them, after the Savior's birth, according to the requirements of the Law of Moses. It was there that Simeon and Anna met them, and thus fulfilled God's promise to the aged Simeon. What if Joseph had never come?

Joseph the Carpenter

Humbly and appreciatively, Joseph accepted the gifts offered by the wise men. What if Joseph had been too proud to take charity – what then?

Just imagine how the course of history would have been altered if Joseph had been slow to wake up, and slow to obey when the angel came and warned him of the approach of Herod's murderous soldiers?

Joseph was submissive to God. He fled into a strange land, taking Mary and the baby, and remained there until the angel bid him return.

True to his role, throughout the Savior's boyhood, Joseph taught Jesus the trade of a carpenter. He loved Him deeply enough to seek Him sorrowing for many days when He disappeared in Jerusalem at the age of twelve.

When the Savior hung upon the cross at the end of His life, He committed the care of His beloved mother into the hands of John the Beloved, one of the apostles. So, where was Joseph? We do not know. But maybe it was the death of Joseph that perfected the Savior's empathy sufficient to bring Him to tears at the death of His friend, Lazarus; or moved Him to restore the life of the daughter of Jairus and the son of the widow of Nain; and enables Him now to comfort us when we lose those that we love. He understands perfectly.

Isaiah spoke of the Savior as "… a man of sorrows, and acquainted with grief…" (Isaiah 53:3). Surely Joseph, who loved Him, could no more have escaped the pain that his son suffered than a parent who sees their child suffer now.

Joseph, the carpenter, blessed not only the lives of Jesus and Mary with his faith and devotion, but indeed all of history. Thanks be to God for the man Joseph and the gifts he gave.

The Witness of the Shepherds

BETHLEHEM *Scriptures: Luke 2*

"And there were in the same country shepherds abiding in the field, keeping watch over their flock by night" (Luke 2:8).

Isaiah spoke of the Messiah as a shepherd feeding His flock and gathering His lambs. Therefore, it was to establish His role as the shepherd of Israel that Jesus was born and announced to the world by Israel's shepherds. Moreover, since Bethlehem was pasture to those lambs destined for sacrifice for the sins of the people in the temple, Jesus, the Lamb of God, was born in Bethlehem among the lambs of God.

"And, lo, the angel of the Lord came upon them, and the glory of the Lord shone round about them: and they were sore afraid" (Luke 2:9).

These were not just men who happened to be in the right place at the right time. They were 'just and holy' men. They were righteous men, who were transfigured before God, and called by Him to prepare Israel to receive the Savior and His words. This was no accident.

"And the angel said unto them, Fear not: for, behold, I bring you good tidings of great joy, which shall be to all people" (Luke 2:10).

'Gospel' means 'good tidings' or 'good news.' Of all that ever has been or ever will be in this world that is called 'news,' this was the greatest news of all! Oh, how great is the importance to make these things known unto the children of men, that they may know that there is no flesh that can dwell in the presence of God, save it be through the merits, mercy, and grace of the Holy Messiah. This was the most important life ever lived, and the most meaningful mission ever given to a man, and now He was here.

"For unto you is born this day in the city of David a Saviour, which is Christ the Lord" (Luke 2:11).

The greatest gift of all Christmas gifts – past, present, and future – was this one. God gave us His son. He is Jehovah, the God of your fathers, and He is mighty to save.

"And this shall be a sign unto you; Ye shall find the babe wrapped in swaddling clothes, lying in a manger" (Luke 2:12).

Think of how this must have sounded to those shepherds. The Savior – a baby? The Messiah – Jehovah – lying in a manger? This is extraordinary! But then again, this was no ordinary baby.

By this sign, by the angel telling them this, not only did the shepherds know Him when they found Him, but in every worthy sense, their faith was confirmed by that sign. They knew Him and they knew what He was the moment they laid eyes on Him.

"And suddenly there was with the angel a multitude of the heavenly host praising God, and saying, Glory to God in the highest, and on earth peace, good will toward men" (Luke 2:13-14).

This was not just joy bursting forth in song. This reveals how Heaven viewed the Savior's coming. It tells what they thought of Him, and what He was here for. Jesus came to earth to glorify the Father, do His will upon the earth, and bring God's peace to every troubled heart. Please note how Jesus was and still is the most joyful of music.

"And they came with haste, and found Mary, and Joseph, and the babe lying in a manger. And when they had seen it, they made known abroad the saying which was told them concerning this child. And all they that heard it wondered at those things which were told them by the shepherds" (Luke 2:16-18).

Do you see it? Do you see why the shepherds are part of that story? They were born to be witnesses. Israel's priests in Jerusalem were the authorized, rightful shepherds who should have announced Him to the world, but they had devoured the flock and lost their place. Therefore, then as now, it is the weak and simple, the shepherds, who are honored to be the Lord's first witnesses.

Why did the people wonder at their words? Well, that's obvious. The Lord often tests our faith in His message by the messenger who delivers it.

Humbly, "… Mary kept all these things, and pondered them in her heart" (Luke 2:19).

Line upon line, Mary learned who her son was, and what He was born to be. She was quick to observe. Mary did not let these events ever dwindle in her memory. Forever, and ever, she kept this first Christmas in her heart, and pondered the real meaning until she understood – as should we. God bless.

THE WISE MEN

BETHLEHEM *Scriptures: Matthew 2*

A wise man is one who has knowledge and understands how best to use it. There is nothing more wise than to find and then follow the Lord Jesus Christ.

After Jesus was born, "...there came wise men from the east to Jerusalem, saying, Where is he that is born King of the Jews? For we have seen His star in the east, and are come to worship Him" (Matthew 2:1-2).

The Bible foretells nothing of a new star, yet somehow these faithful disciples knew it was coming, knew what it meant, and when it appeared they understood it to be the sign of the Messiah. Like all the faithful, they wanted to see Him, be with Him – worship Him. And so, they set out to find Him.

Because light always stirs up darkness, Herod and "all Jerusalem" were "troubled" at the news of the child. Herod "greatly feared" Him as the deliverer spoken of by the prophets, even though He refused to believe and obey. He demanded of the Jews to know where Christ would be born. He was told Bethlehem. Then Herod "called the wise men privily," and learned that the star had appeared almost two years before.

Herod feigned faith, but his intent was to use the Wise Men to find Jesus and kill Him. So he sent them on to Bethlehem, saying, "Go and search diligently for the young child; and when ye have found him, bring me word again that I may come and worship Him also" (Matthew 2:8).

As the Wise Men began the short journey to Bethlehem, the star that had begun their long journey in the east reappeared, and beckoned them to follow.

"They rejoiced with exceedingly great joy" to see it again. It "...went before them until it came and stood over where the young child was" (Matthew 2:9).

That star was for them as Christ is now for us, a heavenly light so far away, and yet so close and personal. "And when they came into the house, they saw the young child with Mary, His mother, and fell down and worshipped Him..." (Matthew 2:11).

There it is! That is why they were called Wise Men. Jesus had "no form nor comeliness," and "no beauty that we should desire Him." These grown and wise, seasoned and mature men fell to their knees before him in reverence and meek adoration. They were truly wise for they knew of Him what man cannot know without revelation. This child was their Savior and Redeemer.

"...When they had opened their treasures, they presented Him gifts; gold, frankincense, and myrrh" (Matthew 2:11), because those who love the Lord give Him all that they have as well as all that they are.

As the Wise Men settled down to sleep that night, they were "warned of God in a dream not to return to Herod." They rose and departed the country another way. An angel of the Lord then appeared to Joseph in a dream saying, "Arise, and take the young child and His mother and flee into Egypt... for Herod will seek the young child to destroy Him'" (Matthew 2:13). The danger was real. Isaiah said Jesus "... would grow up before Him as a tender plant" (Isaiah 53:2).

As a child, Jesus was as subject to cold, hunger, and to death as any other child. When warned of impending danger, immediately Joseph arose and took Jesus and His mother by night and fled into Egypt. Herod was incensed at being so deceived and in an effort to kill the Son of God, he "...sent forth and slew all the children in Bethlehem and in all the coasts thereof from two years old and under..." (Matthew 2:16).

This was the most foolish thing any man could have ever done.

This story is about wise and foolish men.

Fools still ignore and scorn the Son of God.

The wise still seek Him.

If you would be wise in the wisest of all wisdom, "...Ask and it shall be given you; seek, and ye shall find; knock, and it shall be opened unto you" (Matthew 7:7). Remember, just as it was that night for the Wise Men, so will it be for you – the door is still open.

HEROD THE GREAT

JERICHO

We have all heard the Christmas story of the slaughter of the innocents ordered by Herod the Great when Jesus was two-years-old. But, who exactly was Herod and why would he do such a horrendous thing? According to the historical record, the answer is power!

Herod was born about 72 BCE at Idumea, which is south and east of Judea. His parents were of Arab descent. In fact, for those who have been there, Herod's mother may well have been from Petra. Under his father's patronage, Herod first came to power as governor of Galilee when he was 25 years old. He came into prominence when he brutally destroyed bandits in the region.

Herod came to the favorable attention of Rome, and in 39 BCE, he was appointed King of Judea by the Roman Senate. In the subsequent fight for his throne, Herod married Mariamne, the granddaughter of Hyrcanus, the high priest. However, Herod was already married to Doris and had a son. He banished both of them. In 36 BCE, Herod considered his brother-in-law, Aristobulus, as a threat to his throne and ordered him drowned at a party he sponsored. In 29 BCE, Herod became jealous of his wife, Mariamne, and ordered her executed.

Immediately following that, he executed Mariamne's mother, Alexandra, as a threat to his throne. As the years passed, Herod executed another brother-in-law and three sons: Alexander, Aristobulus, and Antipater. All of this says nothing of his cruelty to his own people. As one scholar wrote,

> "The terrible acts of bloodshed which Herod perpetrated in his own family were accompanied by others among his subjects equally terrible, from the number who fell victims to them."

Near the end, Herod became grievously ill with a mysterious affliction known today as "Herod's Evil". It was under the grip of that fatal illness that Herod ordered the babes of Bethlehem to be slain. Canon Frederic Farrar, who wrote The Life of Christ, said:

> "It must have been very shortly after the murder of the innocents that Herod died. Only five days before his death, he had made a frantic attempt at suicide and had ordered the execution of his eldest son, Antipater. His death-bed, which once more reminds us of Henry VIII, was accompanied by circumstances of peculiar horror; and it has been asserted that he died of a loathsome disease, which is hardly mentioned in history, except in the case of men who have been rendered infamous by an atrocity of persecuting zeal.
>
> On his bed of intolerable anguish, in that splendid and luxurious palace which he had built for himself, under the palms of Jericho, [he was] swollen with disease and scorched by thirst, ulcerated externally and glowing inwardly with a soft, slow fire. [Herod was] surrounded by plotting sons and plundering slaves, detesting all and detested by all, longing for death as a release from his tortures, yet dreading it as the beginning of worse terrors, stung by remorse, yet still unslaked with murder, a horror to all around him.
>
> Yet, in his guilty conscience, a worse terror to himself, devoured by the premature corruption of an anticipated grave, eaten of worms as though visibly

smitten by the finger of God's wrath after seventy years of successful villainy, the wretched old man, whom men had called the Great, lay in savage frenzy awaiting his last hour.

As he knew that none would shed one tear for him, he determined that they should shed many for themselves, and issued an order that, under pain of death, the principal families of the kingdom and the chiefs of the tribes should come to Jericho. They came, and then, shutting them in the hippodrome, he secretly commanded his sister Salome that at the moment of his death they should all be massacred. And so, choking as it were with blood, devising massacres in its very delirium, the soul of Herod passed forth into the night.

Power is an addicting drug for which some have sold their souls in infamy to hold. That is the story of Herod the Great.

Sources:

https://en.wikipedia.org/wiki/Herod_the_Great

Smith Comprehensive Dictionary of the Bible, cited in Talmage, Jesus the Christ, p. 101

https://www.churchofjesuschrist.org/study/manual/jesus-the-christ/chapter-8?lang=eng

9

Bethlehem Today

BETHLEHEM

Every year, the Christmas season ends and we start a new year. Each year the songs and stories of Christmas evoke, at least for me, an image of Bethlehem as a quiet, sleepy, pastoral village, surrounded by sheep, illuminated by stars, and watched over by angels. It makes me think of Bethlehem as a place of perfect peace.

To my surprise, when I visited there I learned that today there is a 24-foot concrete wall topped with razor-wire surrounding the city of Bethlehem on three sides. Where Joseph and Mary once entered the city without difficulty, today they couldn't even get in.

There are guards armed with assault rifles that guard the gate of Bethlehem. Israelis cannot get in, and only a few Palestinians are allowed out.

Where once, rumors of miracle babies – John the Baptist and Jesus – spread throughout that area with great speed, now it can take as long as a month just to get a postcard six miles from Bethlehem on the West Bank into Jerusalem.

Where once Bethlehem belonged to the Jews and they were ruled by Rome, now the city belongs primarily to Muslims and they are ruled by Jews. Tragically, out of Bethlehem have come at least a dozen suicide bombers over the years.

In Jesus' day, Bethlehem meant House of Bread, and out of it came Jesus, the Bread of Life, the giver of the abundant life. Today in Bethlehem, unemployment runs rampant and the people are desperate and dependent.

Two thousand years ago, the city was so crowded with people from out of town that the inns were full, and Mary and Joseph could find shelter and comfort only in a stable. Now, the hotels of Bethlehem are nearly empty; few people spend the night there. The residents of the city are prisoners, and refugee camps fringe its borders.

What of that holy stable where the shepherds came in peace and joy, where the Christ Child was born? That site today resembles a stone fortress. Tourists are escorted in and then quickly depart. Three modern Christian churches presently occupy the Church of the Nativity, and they fight continually for dominance over it. The guards, who are placed to protect the Church, watch the priests to keep them from attacking each other.

Bethlehem could be called "the" city of Christians, yet today the Christians are fleeing the city. It was once 90% Christian. Today, it's less than a third, and those numbers are dwindling rapidly.

Ironically, to the Israelis, Christians are Palestinian; and to the Palestinians, Christians are foreigners or infidels. Christians in Bethlehem are simply strangers and foreigners.

Yes, Bethlehem is Christmas, yet the very holiday itself is celebrated on three different days in Bethlehem. It was here that the Prince of Peace came into the world amid tidings of joy and good will – yet there is no peace. Bethlehem is a city of misery and one of the most contentious places on earth. Joy to the world? Bethlehem is a living testament that the joy of Christmas and the message of the Christ are not reaching us.

Hate is still strong, "… and mocks the song of peace on earth, and good will to men" ("I Heard the Bells on Christmas Day").

Bethlehem Today

Therefore, it is vital that we become as children, meek and lowly of heart, so that we may say in June what we sang in December:

> "Be near me, Lord Jesus, I ask Thee to stay
>
> Close by me forever, and love me, I pray.
>
> Bless all the dear children in thy tender care,
>
> And fit us for heaven, to live with Thee there."

(From the Christmas song, "Away in a Manger")

Indeed, let there be peace on earth, and let it begin with me—now!

10

The Prophecy of Simeon

THE TEMPLE IN JERUSALEM *Scriptures: Luke 2*

I have heard it said that if all you know is what you see with your natural eyes and hear with your natural ears, then you will not know very much. Those who live by the Holy Ghost see, hear, and know much more than those of the world can enjoy.

Forty days after the Savior's birth, Joseph and Mary brought Him to the temple in Jerusalem. Ever since the Passover, the firstborn sons in Israel belonged to the Lord. Therefore, Joseph and Mary made an offering in their poverty of two turtledoves to redeem Jesus. To see it another way, Joseph, His father, made a sacrificial offering to redeem his son, just as Heavenly Father would later make a sacrificial offering of His Son and redeem all mankind.

"And, behold, there was a man in Jerusalem whose name was Simeon; and the same man was just and devout, waiting for the consolation of Israel: and the Holy Ghost was upon him. And it was revealed unto him by the Holy Ghost, that he should not see death, before he had seen the Lord's Christ" (Luke 2:25-26).

On that day, the Spirit led Simeon into that crowded temple at the same time that Joseph and Mary were there. With all of Jerusalem as an audience, the Holy Ghost identified Jesus to Simeon. He came straight to Mary, and lifted the baby out of her arms and into his own.

"Lord," he said in humble praise, "now lettest thou thy servant depart in peace, according to thy word. For mine eyes have seen thy salvation, which thou hast prepared before the face of

The Prophecy of Simeon

all the people; a light to lighten the Gentiles, and the glory of thy people Israel" (Luke 2:29-32).

Simeon was exultant. He was thrilled to his soul, and joyously happy, for that for which he had waited for so long had finally come. Joseph and Mary marveled at those things which were spoken by him. Very seldom does the Lord reveal all of His word at once. Line upon line and precept upon precept, revelation comes incrementally and in packets to the faithful. Joseph and Mary were no exception. They too were still learning who their son really was.

At that point, a strange thing happened. Simeon turned to Mary and spoke to and of her sensitive soul.

"… Behold, this child," he said, as if in warning, "is set for the fall and rising again of many in Israel; and for a sign which shall be spoken against" (Luke 2:34).

Your son, Mary, will reveal the hearts of all people. He will be both loved and hated. His name will be had for good and evil among all men. Those who love light and truth will come in reverence to Him, and will rise with Him. Those who love darkness rather than light will be exposed, and they will hate Him, and they will fall.

"Yea," Simeon continued, as if in prophetic illustration, Mary, "a sword shall pierce through thine own soul also" (Luke 2:35). What kind of a statement is that to make to a mother in the joy of a newborn son? No wonder everyone ignores this part of the Christmas story! However, this prophecy embodied the real meaning of Christmas and of the Savior's life.

Gethsemane, Golgotha, and the Garden Tomb give Christmas and the manger its meaning, and its joy, and Simeon, an old man who was about to die, understood that.

All of us have fallen and will fall, but praise God from whom all blessings flow. Joy to the world indeed, for we can rise again! When we see Christmas as Simeon saw it, this season becomes not one of celebration only. It becomes one of worship. The joy and the peace are not seasonal – they last all year. The best gifts become those that express the most love for God and for man.

The Boy Jesus

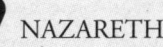 NAZARETH   *Scriptures: Luke 2*

The Lord Jesus Christ was the one perfect being this world has ever known. When He said "follow me," it was not just in where He went, but in the way He went. From His childhood, He was the perfect example.

An angel of the Lord appeared to Joseph in Egypt and told him that it was safe to take Mary and Jesus back to Israel. It was his intention to return to Bethlehem, but when he learned that Herod's son ruled there, he feared going back. Directed again by the angel, he went to an obscure Galilean village called Nazareth (Matthew 2:19-23).

And there, Jesus grew up with his brethren. He was the oldest of five brothers, James, Joses, Simon and Judas, and at least two sisters (Matthew 13:55-56).

At the age of twelve, Jesus traveled with His parents to Jerusalem for the feast of the Passover. When they set out for home, Jesus stayed back. Three days later, they found Him in the Temple, teaching the doctors and answering their questions. It was an amazing spectacle, both to His audience and His parents, to see this mere boy teaching the gospel to the wisest of His day.

"Son," His mother said, "why hast thou thus dealt with us? Behold thy father and I have sought thee sorrowing" (Luke 2:48).

"How is it that ye sought me," he said, "wist ye not that I must be about my father's business?" (Luke 2:49). He had tarried by design to teach and bring souls unto God. Where else should his parents have looked for Him than in the Temple – His Father's house.

Nevertheless, He obeyed His parents and went home with them. By the age of twelve, Jesus knew He was God's son, not Joseph's son. However, Jesus was born with no memory of his former glory. Like every other child, He grew line upon line and precept upon precept, increasing in wisdom, except, He grew until no man on earth was wise enough to teach Him. And yet, as He grew powerful, He also increased in favor with God and man (Luke 2:52).

He always did those things that pleased His Heavenly Father, and consequently, the grace of God was upon Him (Luke 2:40), and never left Him. Similarly, He understood love and by that power men loved Him.

Jesus knew who He was and what He was born to do, and yet for 30 years, He was the carpenter's son, working under Joseph, all the while waiting – preparing, growing in strength, wisdom, and spirituality. When it was time, He came out of Galilee to Jordan, unto John, to be baptized, having prepared Himself spiritually, intellectually, physically, and socially, just as we must do if we would go where He went, and become as He is.

12

Temptation

 WILDERNESS OF TEMPTATION, JUDEAN DESERT SOUTH OF JERUSALEM *Scriptures: Matthew 4, 1 Peter 5*

In the war between good and evil, it is a surety that any man who goes it alone against evil will be pounded and marred as surely as the Savior was when those spikes pierced His flesh. Hence, that you might avoid this, a meaningful story has been preserved.

After Jesus was baptized, the Spirit filled Him and took Him into the wilderness to be with His Father. Fasting for forty days, Jesus communed with the Father in the midst of the beauty and beasts of the desert quiet. He and the Father drew very close. But then, the Spirit withdrew, the Father left Him, and hunger tore at the Savior's body.

It was then that the devil came, as he always comes, desiring to wreck that close relationship wrought by prayer.

"...If thou be the Son of God," Lucifer whispered tauntingly, "command that these stones be made bread" (Matthew 4:3).

It was as if he was saying, "You're the Son of God, aren't you? You don't deserve to suffer like this. You have the power. Make bread! Eat!"

There's nothing wrong with making bread, and there's nothing sinful about eating it either. So, where's the temptation? It is in any action contrary to the will of the Father. You see, God had not yet given the word for Jesus to end His fast. Bread is not wrong unless partaken of at the wrong time.

Thus Jesus said, "...Man shall not live by bread alone, but by every word that proceedeth out of the mouth of God" (Matthew 4:4). Jesus needed to eat, but He needed to obey His Father more.

By this choice can you see that Jesus avoided the very thing that damns most of humanity, namely, trading what we want most forever for what our body demands now?

Why did the Father leave Him? It's because a good man can only be a good man if he chooses good while facing evil. All men, and especially the Son of God, must be fairly offered good and evil, and then choose, of his own free will, between the two.

With that, don't be surprised when it seems you are all alone in your times of tormentous testing. It will feel like it, but I assure you–you're not alone.

The needs and passions of our physical bodies are like electricity. They're very good and very powerful when properly understood and controlled, but are deadly when handled carelessly. It's true that we came here to Earth to get a body and be tested. But you know, so many of the high point questions of that celestial exam deal with the body, so much so that the body might as well be the test of mortality. The scriptures call it chains of darkness, but we call it 'addiction.' Either way, uncontrolled indulgence of the body suspends agency and makes men slaves to the flesh, and tumbleweeds before Lucifer's winds.

It is true that the devil is as a roaring lion, prowling about and "seeking whom he may devour" (1 Peter 5:8). That does not mean we have to be dozing warthogs staked in place and waiting.

We have a Savior who has faced the full fury of the temptations of the body and won. Come to Him – even if that's all the strength you have left. Believe Him and come to Him, and He will help.

13

FRIENDS HELPING FRIENDS

BETHABARA, BEYOND JORDAN   *Scriptures: John 1*

It is friendship that warms hearts and binds together individuals, families, and nations. Friendship is what happens when love is acted upon. Just how important is friendship to the ongoing work of God? Please consider this.

At the beginning of the Savior's ministry, Jesus came to John the Baptist to receive baptism. John bore witness of Him as the Messiah to all who would listen. One day, not long after that, John saw Jesus walking nearby, and turning to two of his disciples he said, "Behold the Lamb of God!" (John 1:36).

Curious, the two disciples began to follow Jesus. He turned and saw them following Him and said, "What seek ye?" They said unto him, "Rabbi, where dwellest thou?" He answered them, "Come and see" (John 1:38-39).

They went with Him to where He was staying, and since it was late in the day, they spent the night.

The scriptures are silent as to what happened that evening, but the conversation must have been glorious, because the next day Andrew, one of the two, set out immediately to find his brother Simon.

"...We have found the Messiah...," Andrew announced to Simon (John 1:41).

Then he brought him to Jesus. When Jesus saw him, he welcomed him saying, "...Thou art Simon, the son of Jona: thou shalt be called Cephas, which is by interpretation a stone" (John 1:42).

Friends Helping Friends

The next day Jesus went into Galilee, and He found Phillip. No sooner was Phillip convinced that Jesus was the Messiah than he went out and found his best friend Nathaniel. "...We have found him, of whom Moses in the law, and the prophets, did write, Jesus of Nazareth, the son of Joseph," Phillip declared (John 1:45).

Nathaniel found that just a little hard to believe. "...Can there any good thing come out of Nazareth?" he asked (John 1:46).

Philip's response was the answer of the ages for all seekers when he replied, "Come and see" (John 1:46).

The moment Jesus saw Nathaniel, He said, "Behold, an Israelite indeed, in whom [there] is no guile!" (John 1:47). From that point forward, Nathaniel became one of those who left all and followed the Master.

Friends bring friends to Christ. They always have – they always will, and thereby the Kingdom of God on the earth grows. Men are saved and the work rolls forward. Moreover, just as this story illustrates, you don't need to worry about your friends. It doesn't matter who or what your friend is, the Savior will welcome him or her and put them to work. So, go and tell a friend what you've found.

14

Water Into Wine

 CANA   *Scriptures: John 2*

There is great meaning sometimes in what appears to be the most mundane.

The beginning of the Savior's miracles was the turning of the water into wine.

There was a wedding, and Jesus and His disciples were invited to it. Sometime late in the festivities, Mary, His mother, came to Him and said, "...They have no wine" (John 2:3).

It was an implied request, and Jesus answered, "Woman, what have I to do with thee? Mine hour is not yet come" (John 2:4).

In essence, He was saying, "Mother, I will do anything I can for you."

Mary turned to the servants and said to them, "...Whatsoever He saith unto you, do it" (John 2:5).

With His disciples watching, Jesus asked the servants to fill some nearby water pots. The amount of water in those six pots would have been between 100 and 150 gallons. Evidently, this was a well-attended party!

Once they finished filling them up, and without any fuss or fanfare, Jesus said simply, "...Draw out now, and bear unto the governor of the feast..." (John 2:8).

The servants obeyed, and brought the new wine to the ruler of the feast. He tasted it and exclaimed, "...Every man at the beginning doth set forth good wine; and when men have well drunk, then that which is worse: but thou hast kept the good wine until now" (John 2:10).

This first miracle passed quietly. There is no evidence that the guests knew what had happened – but the disciples did. To them it manifested forth His glory and strengthened their faith.

Now, doctrinally speaking, it is no accident that the beginning of the Savior's miracles involved water. When Moses changed water to blood, he proved that God was with him. When Jesus turned water to wine, He proved He was God. Moses parted the sea and walked through it; Jesus calmed the sea and walked on it. By these miracles, Jesus proved that He was the long-awaited prophet like unto Moses.

Like water, most of us are pretty common, ordinary, and unremarkable. Yet, when the Lord sets His mind to change us, we too can become something good – a miracle. Just as Jesus made water into wine, He will make bad men good, and good men perfect – even you!

15

Come to Jesus

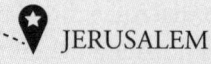 JERUSALEM   *Scriptures: John 5*

There is no prison worse than the one we put ourselves in.

In ancient Jerusalem, there was a man beside the pool of Bethesda. He was called 'impotent' because he had no power. He couldn't walk and he was helpless. John made mention of him in the fifth chapter. He was terribly afflicted and scarcely able to move. He languished in lonely misery beside that pool, waiting with many others for the water to stir, and hoping that by some miracle he, this time, might be the first to enter the angel's waters and be healed.

It had been thirty-eight years since his sins so entrapped and afflicted him. Can you imagine? For thirty-eight desperate years he had done all he could to free himself of his physical, emotional, and spiritual prison – and to no avail. Where was his hope?

Then one day, a stranger entered the porches of Bethesda and walked among the multitude of sick folk. Coming to the man, Jesus knew him and He stopped.

"…Wilt thou be made whole?" the Savior asked (John 5:6).

"… Sir," the crippled man respectfully replied, "I have no man, when the water is troubled, to put me into the pool: but while I am coming another steppeth down before me" (John 5:7).

"Rise," the Master said, "Take up thy bed and walk" (John 5:8).

Come to Jesus

For the first time in almost 40 long years, the impotent man stood; he walked, and was whole. Having no power to come to the Savior, Jesus came to Him – and so He continues to do.

The Savior has said repeatedly, "Come unto me."

There are some who don't know they should come, and there are some who think this journey can be made whenever and however they choose, or that it's a one-time trip.

They are all mistaken! The journey to Jesus takes a lifetime and beyond. None of us has any more power to come to Jesus than He gives us, nor can we come any closer to Him than He allows.

Praise be to God! He loves us – all of us. He wants all of us near Him – in Him. He will at the appointed time come for each of us, even and especially for those humble prisoners who want so desperately to come and be closer to Him, but they just don't know how.

Be patient, and do your best. He is watching, and He will come!

Photina the Samaritan Woman

 SAMARIA   *Scriptures: John 4*

The Samaritans of Jesus' day were a people more despised than a gentile. They were considered a mongrel, mixed race of people, dating back more than seven centuries. Not only was their blood mixed, but their religious traditions were adulterated as well.

The Jews had no dealings with the Samaritans. Hence, it was a remarkable thing when the Lord's disciples came up over the hill and saw their Lord talking with the Samaritan woman at Jacob's well, near the present day city of Nablus.

The Rabbis of the day would not so much as walk on Samaritan soil, let alone speak with a Samaritan or partake of their food and drink. Yet, here was Jesus not only talking to a Samaritan, but a woman no less. Most Rabbis would not condescend to teach religion one-on-one to a woman, but here was Jesus teaching her and bearing witness to her that he was the Messiah. Even the woman was astounded that Jesus would speak to her and ask for a drink of water. This was not just any woman, as evidenced by what came out of their conversation.

To this woman accustomed to the daily drudgery of walking to the well, drawing her water and returning, Jesus offered living water. "Whosoever drinketh of the water which I shall give him shall never thirst," Jesus promised, "but the water that I shall give him shall be in him a well of water springing up into everlasting life" (John 4:14). "Sir," she said, "Give me of this water, that I thirst not, neither come hither to draw" (John 4:15).

Jesus then told her to go and call her husband, to which the woman responded that she had no husband. "Thou hast well said," Jesus replied, "For thou hast had five husbands; and he whom thou now hast is not thy husband: in that saidst thou truly" (John 4:18).

Evidently, this woman had been married five times and divorced each time for unfaithfulness, and was presently living in sin with another man. She was a Samaritan, a woman, and evidently an adulteress, shamed and unworthy even among her own people, and yet, none of that mattered to the Master. Her soul was precious enough that he took time for her, taught her, and converted her, and she became His witness. Tradition holds to this day that her name was Photina and that she died a martyr for Christ in Rome.

This story is one of the most human in the New Testament because it teaches that Jesus cares for his sheep individually, especially the lost ones.

The Nobleman's Son

 CANA *Scriptures: John 4*

One day Jesus came into the little town of Cana of Galilee, where He was met by a nobleman. It seems that this man's son was dying, and he desperately begged Jesus to come down and heal him. The son was 20 miles away in Capernaum. What the father wanted was for Jesus, right then and there, to travel to Capernaum and presumably lay His hands on the boy and heal him.

What happened next in the story is intriguing. Instead of commending the man for his faith in coming in the first place, Jesus chided him saying, "...Except ye see signs and wonders, ye will not believe" (John 4:48).

The man was not offended, but rather persisted saying, "...Sir, come down ere my child die" (John 4:49).

Why did Jesus rebuke him? It's obvious he had faith. Maybe this man is like so many of us. He came to Jesus for help, telling Jesus where, when, and how that help was to be delivered. In his mind, unless Jesus was physically there in Capernaum, the boy couldn't be healed, but Jesus was so much more than this man ever imagined. He was Lord of the universe, had all power and knowledge, and with Him all things were, and still are, possible. It seems audacious to put God in a box by limiting what He can do, what, when, and how.

Jesus stretched the man's faith and said, "...Go thy way; thy son liveth..." (John 4:50).

The Nobleman's Son

The man believed the Lord's healing words, and he set out for home. On the way, he was met by his servants announcing that his son was indeed on the mend. When he asked them when the boy began to heal, he was informed that it was the seventh hour, the exact same moment that Jesus had spoken.

He went for a miracle of healing and returned converted to the Gospel – he and all his household. He, like so many of us, can get far more than we set out for if we'll just remember there are no limits to God! He can do anything for us He wants to if we will let Him. His ways are not our ways. They're better!

I think it is wise to remember that to surrender our stubborn will to God in faith is to set us free.

JESUS VISITS NAZARETH

 NAZARETH

Scriptures: Proverbs 18, Luke 4Him.

Wisdom says, "He that answereth a matter before he heareth it, it is folly and shame unto him" (Proverbs 18:13).

A mind closed is a heart hardened, and a hardened heart is a lost opportunity – for example:

Full of the Spirit, Jesus came out of the wilderness after His baptism and returned to His hometown of Nazareth. When something wonderful happens to us, it's often with us that we want to tell our friends and family. They're the ones we want to share it with.

Jesus came to Nazareth, His home town. He stood up in Church and read these words from Isaiah 61 saying, "The Spirit of the Lord is upon me, because he hath anointed me to preach the gospel to the poor; he hath sent me to heal the brokenhearted, to preach deliverance to the captives, and recovering of sight to the blind, to set at liberty them that are bruised, To preach the acceptable year of the Lord" (Luke 4:18-19).

Every eye in that congregation was fixed on Jesus. They had heard the rumors of Him, and now they waited to see what He would say next.

Jesus opened His mouth and said simply, "...This day is this scripture fulfilled in your ears" (Luke 4:21).

At that moment, Jesus was making them the greatest offer of all eternity. He was the promised Messiah, and they would have a privileged place to know Him as few others could – if they would believe.

The next explosive moments, however, must have been some of the most painful of the Master's life. At first, the crowd began to murmur against His supposed presumptuousness, but then He spoke again and told them He could do no miracle for them, for they had less faith than the gentiles.

With that, the congregation came apart! They were filled with wrath, and right there, they grabbed Him, hauled Him out of their city, and attempted to murder Him by throwing Him off the cliff on which their city was built. With a power greater than they could understand, He passed "...through the midst of them went his way" (Luke 4:30).

They did not – they would not listen! What they thought they knew of Jesus overpowered their reason and closed their minds to who He really was and what they could have known about He was offering to set them free as they had never been free, give them peace, joy, power, and wealth such as they had never known, nor could they comprehend. But instead, they chose misery and damnation for their rash judgment. It was this that caused Jesus to say, "...No prophet is accepted in his own country" (Luke 4:24).

I pray that we might be wiser than the people that day in the synagogue in Nazareth. Allow the Almighty to make someone we know greater than we thought they could be. It may be that from those we least expect we will hear the most powerful things. Do not let someone's past hold hostage their future.

19

THE POWER OF HIS WORD

CAPERNAUM *Scriptures: Matthew 8, Mark 1*

Talk, talk, and more talk! We live in a world these days where problems seem to be solved by throwing words at them, and it doesn't seem to be working. With all this noise, wouldn't it be wonderful to hear a word these days that has real power?

One Sabbath Day in Capernaum, Jesus went to synagogue and taught. The people were astonished at His words. It wasn't just what He said, but it was the power that His words had upon their hearts. What he said seemed to emanate authority and believability, and moved the people to action.

During His teaching, a man suddenly stood up and cried out, "Let us alone; what have we to do with thee, thou Jesus of Nazareth? Art thou come to destroy us? I know thee who thou art, the Holy One of God" (Mark 1:24).

Jesus rebuked the man right there on the spot commanding, "...Hold thy peace, and come out of him" (Mark 1:25).

To the astonishment of everyone present, the unclean spirit that was in the man threw him into violent convulsions, and then came out of him. The man was unharmed. The people who were watching were amazed and spoke among themselves, "...What a word is this" (Luke 4:36).

As those unusual services ended, the word of what had happened in church that day spread throughout the community. Jesus meanwhile, went to Peter's house. Upon entering, they asked Him to minister to Peter's mother-in-law. She was sick with a great fever. He came, took her by the

The Power of His Word

hand, spoke a word, and instantly she was healed. She arose from her sickbed and ministered to them.

That same evening after sunset, another remarkable thing happened. All the people of the city gathered together at the place where Jesus was. They brought Him all that were diseased, and those that were possessed with devils. Even though Jesus may have wanted time alone with His friends, or perhaps sleep, He nonetheless welcomed them, and laid His hands on every one of them, and healed them!

By the power of His word, Matthew 8:17 says, that He took their infirmities and bore their sicknesses.

Talk is not cheap when it's Jesus talking. There was power in His word then, and there still is – both when He speaks it, and when it is spoken by His authorized servants.

With all the words we will hear today, it is His word that comforts most and causes change. Lord help us first to find His word, and then do what it takes to hear Him.

20

The Palsied Man and His Friends

CAPERNAUM

Scriptures: Matthew 9, Mark 2, Luke 5, James 5

It seems that when I kneel down to pray, the faces of a lot of people that I care about who are in trouble come to my mind, and a lot of my time in prayer is spent for them, hoping beyond hope that Heavenly Father will bless them because of my meager faith and my much concern. I'm sure it's the same with you.

Do you sometimes find yourself wondering if it's doing any good? Will He really help them just because you ask Him to? Is He really listening? Are your feeble efforts with them and with Him making any difference at all?

If any of these questions have been yours, would you consider the following story?

On one of those rare occasions when the Master was at home in Capernaum, word spread quickly throughout the community that He was there, and a crowd came together – so large a crowd in fact that they filled His house to overflowing. To those close enough to hear, which evidently was not all, Jesus taught the Gospel.

Four men were seen approaching the house carrying a sort of portable bed, upon which lay a man who was paralyzed. They tried to enter the house and get to Jesus, but they could not for the crowd. Selflessly determined, these four men hefted their helpless friend up onto the flat roof of the house, and they tore the roof apart – creating a hole, and then lowered their friend through the hole right into the middle of the crowd near Jesus. With compassion, Jesus bade the man to be of good cheer, forgave his sins, and healed his paralysis.

What impresses me most about this story is a little detail that Matthew, Mark, and Luke all record (Matthew 9:2, Mark 2:1-5, Luke 5:18-20).

Mark's words were, "When Jesus saw their faith" (Mark 2:5) not 'his faith,' 'their faith.'

In other words, we have here a man in the spiritual bondage of sin, and the physical bondage of paralysis, who is healed – yes – by his own faith, but in great measure by the faith and the determination of those who loved him and were willing to sacrifice for him.

The next time you wonder if your pitiful prayers are doing any good, please remember this statement from the apostle Paul, "...the effectual fervent prayer of a righteous man availeth much" (James 5:16) – and so it does.

The Paradox of Joy

Scriptures: Matthew 9, Luke 18, 1 John 4

Our Heavenly Father gave us life that we might find joy. All that He does is to lead us to joy. It's our consummate purpose in life and in eternity. Ironically, it's in the obtaining of joy where saints and sinners so radically diverge. While a sinner will seek joy for himself by helping himself, a saint will find joy when he lives to bring it to others, as illustrated by this story.

Jesus was walking by and saw a man named Matthew sitting at the receipt of custom. Matthew was a tax collector, a publican, one of the most hated and despised of all men among the Jews. Publicans usually were Jews that worked for Rome brokering taxes. As such, they were detested as traitors and parasites, living off the lifeblood of their own people.

The Savior walked past Matthew, and said to him simply, "…Follow me…" (Matthew 9:9).

Matthew was a devout Jew and a student of the scriptures. He arose, and followed the Savior. That evening, Matthew hosted a celebratory dinner at his home, and invited the Master to attend. With His disciples and friends, Jesus feasted with Matthew and his friends. The Pharisees came by, and in haughty self-righteousness, looked upon the happy gathering and scorned Jesus.

"…Why eateth your Master with publicans and sinners?" (Matthew 9:11) they said to His disciples.

What were they really saying? – that someone of Jesus' stature shouldn't keep company with such an inferior lot of men

The Paradox of Joy

as tax collectors and sinners? He was, as they considered themselves, too good for them. An attitude like that is based on hate and fear – fear of men. It's not based on love and faith in God.

The New Testament states that "…perfect love casteth out fear…" (1 John 4:18).

It is when we are insecure in our faith and our position that we fear other men – what they may do to us – and we shun them or condemn them.

Jesus overheard that statement, and He said to them, "They that be whole need not a physician, but they that are sick" (Matthew 9:12). This meant if the Pharisees considered themselves spiritually whole and healthy, then He couldn't help them. The publicans and the sinners knew they were spiritually ill, and they came to Jesus for help. They were therefore in reality more healthy before God than the Pharisees were.

If we are confident that we are very righteous before God, it is likely that we're probably worse off than the man who knows he's a sinner and is pleading for forgiveness (Luke 18:9 -14).

The Savior recognized that His physician's metaphor had probably escaped them, and so He said, "Go ye and learn what that meaneth," – and then He added this: "I will have mercy, and not sacrifice: for I am not come to call the righteous, but sinners to repentance" (Matthew 9:13).

When He said "I will have mercy and not sacrifice", the words 'will have' translate as 'desire', meaning to 'desire mercy, and not sacrifice.' It is as though Jesus was saying to those Pharisees, "I want all of you to have mercy and not sacrifice any man. Welcome all men into your company, and be like me in order to help them."

Please consider that when Jesus said, "Come unto me," did He ever say, "except you, or you?" In turning others away, we turn God away from us. In hoarding our happiness, we lose it. Our joy will be as great as we labor to bring it to others.

The Withered Hand

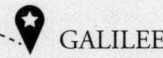 GALILEE   *Scriptures: Matthew 12, Mark 3, Luke 6*

Fresh from an encounter with the Pharisees, Jesus came out of the fields and entered the synagogue. He stood up and began to teach. There were Pharisees in the audience, bent on accusing him. Also, there was a man in the congregation that had a withered right hand. The man was bait. The Pharisees watched Jesus to see if he would heal the man on the Sabbath Day. By their thinking, healing on the Sabbath was work, and violated the Sabbath.

Jesus continued to preach until they suddenly and impatiently interrupted him.

"...Is it lawful to heal on the Sabbath days?" they asked (Matthew 12:10).

It was a trap. If he said yes, he would be defying rabbinical tradition. If he said no, He would be contradicting his own actions. Jesus was always the master of every situation.

He said to the man with the withered hand, "...Rise up, and stand forth..." (Luke 6:8).

The man did so. Then Jesus turned to the Pharisees.

"...I will ask you one thing;" He said. "Is it lawful on the Sabbath days to do good, or to do evil? to save life, or to destroy it?" (Luke 6:9).

That one question of His not only made theirs look utterly absurd, but overturned the rabbinical traditions of the Jewish Sabbath.

The Pharisees could not answer; they just stared at him; they did not dare say anything. In anger, Jesus "...looked round about on them, being grieved for the hardness of their hearts…" (Mark 3:5).

Then He said to the man with the withered hand, "...Stretch forth thine hand," and when he did, it "was restored whole as the other" (Mark 3:5).

This deliberate act of defiance enraged the Pharisees! They left the meeting and immediately began to conspire how they could murder the Savior.

I suppose it still angers Jesus when we, like those Pharisees, care more about being right than doing right. Thank the Lord for those people today who clearly know what is right, and then have the courage to do it.

23

Skeptics and the Faithful

 CAPERNAUM   *Scriptures: Luke 7*

I speak to those who pride themselves on being skeptics.

Jesus came into Capernaum near the beginning of His ministry and was approached by the Elders of the Jews. They asked Him to come and heal a man who was about to die. The ailing man was the servant of a local centurion. A centurion was a Roman military officer in command of a hundred men. This centurion seems different than most soldiers we read about among the Jews in that he was a man of compassion. Even though he was the conqueror, he loved the Jews and built them a synagogue for worship.

Therefore, when the centurion's servant became ill, the Jews told him of Jesus, and His marvelous power to heal. The centurion believed the word of the Jews, and asked them to go to Jesus and request that He come and heal his servant.

Now please note: The Roman commander is asking on behalf of his servant, not himself. The Jews were eager to comply. They found Jesus and earnestly pleaded with Him to come, "saying, "…That he was worthy for whom he should do this" (Luke 7:4).

The Savior agreed. However, before He could reach the home of the centurion, the centurion reconsidered, and he sent friends to the Savior saying,

"Lord, trouble not thyself: for I am not worthy that thou shouldest enter under my roof: neither thought I myself worthy to come unto thee: but say in a word, and my servant shall be healed. For I also am a man set under authority, having under me soldiers, and I say unto one, Go, and he goeth; and to another, Come, and he cometh; and to my servant, Do this, and he doeth it" (Luke 7:6-8).

When the Savior heard this, 'He marveled' at this most meek and lowly man. And then He turned to those who were walking with Him and He said for all to hear,

"...I have not found so great faith, no, not in Israel" (Luke 7:9).

When I read this, I marveled, because I want to be that kind of a man of faith. Where and how did this centurion demonstrate such commendable faith?

I think this is what it is: When the Roman centurion's servant became ill, and the Jews told him about Jesus, he heard that word, and he believed it implicitly. There's no evidence that he did anything but just believe it and then he acted on it by asking Jesus to come.

However, the soldier knew who he was and considered himself unworthy to stand in the presence of the Son of God. The humility of knowing our proper place in the presence of Jesus pleases God. It was in effect as though that centurion was saying, "We are both men of authority. I command soldiers and servants, and they obey me. You command heaven, earth, and angels, and they obey you. I recognize your authority. Speak now on behalf of my servant and no matter where you are, you will be obeyed and he will be healed."

What faith! This man was no skeptic! He heard the word about Jesus; he believed it without question, and acted on it without doubt. He needed no miracles and no great time to pray and find out. He just believed it!

Skeptics and the Faithful

The Savior still moves in power among us. There are those who speak of Him meekly and with authority. Their words can awaken faith and lead to miracles – if we believe. No skeptic will ever find such power – for where skeptics are, faith is not.

24

The Widow of Nain

 NAIN   *Scriptures: Luke 7*

To have compassion is to feel an emotion that combines love and pity. This story is about the compassion of Jesus Christ, and when and where it was seen.

One day the Savior was approaching a beautiful mountain village called Nain. A large crowd accompanied Him, including many of His disciples. As they neared, they came upon a funeral procession. Many of the people filed in mourning with the grieving mother. The man being buried was her only son, and she, tragically, was a widow.

Jesus saw her and perceived the situation immediately. As always, concerned with the plight of the widow, the Savior was filled with tender compassion for her and said, "...Weep not" (Luke 7:13).

He turned from her and "...came and touched the bier: and they that bare him stood still. And He said, Young man, I say unto thee, arise" (Luke 7:14).

The dead man sat up and began to speak. Luke then records these meaningful words, "...And he delivered him to his mother" (Luke 7:15). Can you imagine? What a gift of joy He gave that woman!

A worshipful reverence came upon the people and they glorified God and proclaimed that "...God hath visited his people" (Luke 7:16).

Step back from the story for just a moment. Why did Jesus do this? Did the Savior perform such miracles every time there was a need? No, He did not. Why was this lost son returned to the widow? The record says that "...He had compassion on her" (Luke 7:13). He felt sorry for her, and giving her back her son was the greatest eternal good at that moment.

It was the Widow of Nain who was singled out and so blessed. We do not know all the reasons why this story ended so happily when others did not and have not. In this life, maybe we'll never know. But know this – God does not do anything, save it be for the benefit of the world. He always does the greatest good. He is always just.

Some of us don't get the miracles we want when we want them. Does He care about us any less? Absolutely, not! His love and His compassion for us are perfect and ever-present. The time will come when you and I will all see the salvation of the Lord, and confess before God that His judgments are just. But for now, let us be patient until we are perfected in Christ Jesus, and allowed to see as the Father does.

25

THE WEEPING WOMAN

Scriptures: Luke 7

Can anyone truly love the Savior, and know Him if they have never needed him?

Early in the Savior's ministry, He was invited to the house of Simon the Pharisee who seemed, even in the invitation, motivated by an arrogant curiosity about the Master. Simon disdainfully neglected the usual social customs afforded an honored guest.

During the course of the meal, while reclining feet out on couches around the table, a woman entered and stood at the feet of the Savior. Without a word, she fell at His feet weeping, and began kissing His feet, bathing them with her tears, and wiping them with her hair.

Simon, knowing something of the woman's sinful reputation, scorned the Master in His thoughts, and watched the proceedings with unspoken contempt. Discerning those sin-darkened thoughts, Jesus defended the woman's actions and rebuked the self-righteous, judgmental Pharisee, teaching him with penetrating clarity,

"… to whom little is forgiven, the same loveth little" (Luke 7:47).

To the penitent, grateful woman, and with tender mercy, the Master declared,

"… Thy sins are forgiven (Luke 7:48). "…Thy faith hath saved thee; go in peace" (Luke 7:50).

When our love and faith in the Savior of the world drives us weeping to our knees, seeking His power to forgive, we too can then come to truly love Him and know something of the joy of His abundant mercy.

26

IN THE BOAT WITH US

 SEA OF GALILEE Scriptures: Matthew 8, Mark 4, Luke 8

The Sea of Galilee lies about 680 feet below sea level, making it the second lowest point on the earth's surface. The mountains around it rise to an elevation above 2,000 feet. The temperatures at the lake's surface get very hot and when cooler air sweeps down from the Golan Heights, it can cause very violent winds over the lake's surface.

Jesus had passed the day teaching near the shore of the lake at Capernaum. As evening came, he said to the disciples, "...let us pass over unto the other side" (Mark 4:35).

As they started across the lake, Jesus moved to the back of the little boat and lay down on a pillow and fell asleep. Suddenly, an unusually violent storm of wind came down on the lake and the sea rose. Huge waves began to break over the gunwales of the small boat, filling it with water until it was on the verge of sinking.

The disciples were experienced fishermen. They knew the lake, yet the storm was bad enough that they were terrified. They fought the storm, bailing the boat until all seemed lost. They came to Jesus and awoke Him crying, "...Master, carest thou not that we perish?" (Mark 4:38).

The Savior arose and immediately took in the situation. As the disciples looked on, he stood and rebuked the wind, saying unto the sea, "...Peace, be still..." (Mark 4:39). Instantly, the wind ceased and there followed a great calm.

He then turned to them and said, "...Why are ye so fearful? How is it that ye have no faith?" (Mark 4:40).

The scriptures say, "They feared exceedingly" (Mark 4:41). They said to one another, "What manner of man is this? For He commandeth even the winds and waters, and they obey Him" (Luke 8:25).

Jesus looked like every other man, talked, walked, and acted like every other mortal, but He was so much more than they expected. What man in their world presumed to command the wind and sea, and was obeyed? He may not have looked like much, but He was much more than they could comprehend.

Today, we are in the middle of the deep waters of mortality and threatening tempests are roaring all around us. Fear is pandemic across the nations and men's hearts are failing them – BUT NOT YOU! It is part of the plan that we do all we can to keep rowing and bailing – moving forward, but as a gentle reminder – don't forget He is in the boat with us and can and will help.

27

JAIRUS

CAPERNAUM *Scriptures: Matthew 9, Mark 5, Luke 8*

On one occasion, as the Master and His disciples beached a small boat near Capernaum, He was met by Jairus, the ruler of the synagogue in Capernaum. Jairus' twelve-year-old daughter was dying. We're not told why, only that the onward march of nature that brings death eventually to us all was nigh to claiming this daughter so dearly loved by her father. Desperate to stay nature's course, Jairus asked the Master to intercede, saying, "...My little daughter lieth at the point of death: I pray thee, come and lay thy hands on her that she may be healed; and she shall live" (Mark 5:23).

Recognizing that this was real faith, Jesus went with him. While en route, however, they were met by messengers from Jairus' house, announcing to him that which he least wanted to hear. His daughter had died. Overhearing that dread declaration, Jesus bolstered the grieving father's faith. "...Be not afraid," He comforted, "only believe" (Mark 5:36).

When they arrived at the house, Jesus excused the paid professional mourners who scorned Him as they exited. Their noise was an irksome disruption to the Spirit of the Lord. Then, taking with him only Peter, James, and John, and the damsel's parents, Jesus entered the death chamber. Can you imagine being one of those parents, and the hope you have burning inside of you that Jesus can help?

Taking the girl by the hand He said, "...Damsel, I say unto thee, arise" (Mark 5:41).

Immediately, she arose, and even more, she walked. I can only imagine the inexpressible joy of those parents. I think I can imagine a warm, tender smile on the face of the Master as He witnessed their joyful reunion. After charging them with secrecy that they tell no one of the miracle, He commanded them to feed their daughter and restore her bodily strength.

I love this story. It's beautiful. I wonder how many times nature dictated a disaster to befall our loved ones, and it has been averted because you and I prayed, and called down the powers of a loving God – and He interceded and saved them. How many priceless blessings have you and I received in such a manner and never knew we had? I guess I'm just simple-minded enough to believe that this has happened many times for you and for me. I would hope that we would never underestimate the power of prayer for those we love, that we would never stop praying for them, and thereby placing our loved ones under the umbrella of a loving God's care each day.

28

Close Enough to Touch

Scriptures: Matthew 9, Mark 5, Luke 8

There are some problems which arise in our lives that are just beyond the scope of our ability to solve. I think a wise and loving Heavenly Father has made sure of that. Why? Perhaps it is because if we could solve every problem, answer every question, and cope with every crisis ourselves, what need would we have of Him? There is a much better world than this one waiting for those who in their extremity reach out for His power, as this story attests.

Thronged by a crowd, Jesus followed the anxious Jairus on an errand to heal his dying daughter. Within that crowd was a woman afflicted with an incurable disease. In seeking a cure, she had spent all her fortune, and now, was not healed, but rather more sickly than ever.

Somehow, she learned of the great healer and was determined to go to Him. Because of the nature of her illness, she was ashamed to ask for His help.

As Jesus passed in the crowd with Jairus, she said to herself, "If I may but touch [the hem of] his garment, I shall be whole" (Matthew 9:21).

She pushed her way through the crowd, and from behind she touched the Master's robe. Immediately, there was a tangible surge of power that flowed throughout her body. She was fully healed from that very moment, and she knew it!

Filled with emotion and gratitude, she dropped back into the crowd out of sight. Jesus however stopped, turned around, and scanned the crowd.

"...Who touched me?..." He asked (Luke 8:45).

In effect, Peter said to Him, "There are all these people pushing and shoving, and you ask who touched me?"

Jesus made it clear that this touch was different from any other. "...I perceive," He said, "that virtue is gone out of me" (Luke 8:46).

The woman, knowing that she was discovered, came forward, fell at His feet, and confessed what she had done. With kindness and tenderness, the Master commended her for her faith.

"...Daughter," He said, "be of good comfort: thy faith hath made thee whole; go in peace" (Luke 8:48).

This woman felt unworthy of Him, yet she compelled herself forward, driven by an overwhelming sense that she simply had nowhere else to go.

That is how we exercise faith. We push ourselves toward Him, especially when we don't feel like it. He has power! As we come to Him, His power comes to us – the power to heal, the power to change, but only if we will come close enough to touch.

29

Faith to Walk on Water

 THE SEA OF GALILEE   *Scriptures: Matthew 14, Mark 6, John 6*

Have you ever felt that your faith was just not enough to handle this stressful world? I have, and that's why this story gives me hope. The Lord is the power here, we are not.

Jesus came walking on the Sea of Galilee in the fourth watch or sometime around 3:00 in the morning. The disciples saw Him across the waves in the darkness and cried out in terror, thinking it was a spirit or a ghost.

Jesus bade them "...Be of good cheer; it is I; be not afraid" (Matthew 14:27).

The voice and the form were familiar but still, Peter was not sure.

"...Lord," he said, "if it be thou, bid me come unto thee on the water" (Matthew 14:28).

This was a bold request. Jesus' answer was both an invitation and a stretching. He said simply, "Come" (Matthew 14:29).

Peter did it. He walked on the water. Somehow, as long as his gaze was fixed upon the Lord, his faith was intact, and an inexplicable power supported him across the waves. However, the scripture says, "But when he saw the wind and the waves boisterous, he was afraid; and beginning to sink, cried, Lord, save me" (Matthew 14:30).

Why did he sink? What cut the thread of power that had supported him? It was doubt and fear! When he looked away and let fear supplant his faith in the Lord, he lost power and began to sink – but the Lord was there in his moment of weakness. The Lord stretched forth his hand, caught Peter, and lifted him back up on top of the water. Together they returned to the boat. Amazingly, the winds ceased and there followed a great calm.

In that moment immediately after Jesus had caught Peter, He said to him, "...Oh thou of little faith, wherefore didst thou doubt?" (Matthew 14:31). Jesus understood perfectly well why Peter had doubted. His question was less a query of cause and more a question of Peter's choice. Peter had surrendered to fear.

Some may think that Peter failed – again. But did he – really? His effort increased his faith, and with the Master's gentle correction, he would succeed again.

So it is with us. Our faith may falter for a time, and the trials of this stormy world may threaten to drown us. If we keep our eyes fixed resolutely on Him and go forward, His power will support us. We will stumble, sink, falter, and momentarily fail, but if we reach up for Him with all the desperation of a drowning man, not only will He come to us, but He will bring a great calm to our hearts. He is our power – here and hereafter.

30

That Day in Gennesaret

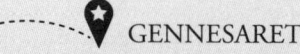 GENNESARET *Scriptures: Matthew 14, Mark 6*

This story is directed to the men and boys of God.

There never lived a man more useful to our Father in Heaven, more productive with his life than the Lord Jesus Christ. He was in every sense of the word "powerful."

For example, one day Jesus and His disciples crossed the Sea of Galilee into an area on the northwestern shore called Gennesaret. As the boat drew to shore, Jesus stepped out, and instantly someone recognized Him. What happens next is astounding.

Those who recognized Him – who knew Him – scattered excitedly, running through the countryside spreading the word that "the healer" had come. From all directions, the people came eagerly, or perhaps desperately, bringing those who were sick and afflicted. Those who could not come under their own power were carried in their beds to meet Jesus. This was from their point of view an opportunity not to be missed.

As Jesus walked – and can you imagine this? The sick and afflicted lined the streets before Him and pleaded for the opportunity to simply touch him, even if it was only the border of his coat, and of course He let them. As each person touched Him, they were healed – made perfectly whole!

Those who came in contact with Jesus felt the power in Him. He inspired confidence, comfort, and faith, just by his very presence. He was different from other men – more pure, more powerful. People sensed that and were drawn to Him, not because He had empty charisma, but because they knew

He could help them in ways no other person could. Can you imagine what it would have been like that day to walk down that street with Him? Imagine if we could have been in His powerful presence and felt His love and comfort.

Why can't there be such men and events like that today? I believe there can. The Lord and the world need men of such power and purity today. Not only is it possible, but given enough faith in Him, it is inevitable! It is, after all, brethren, what we were born to be!

THE BREAD OF LIFE

CAPERNAUM   *Scriptures: Matthew 14, John 6*

As the second Passover of the Lord's ministry drew near, word reached Him that John the Baptist, his friend and forerunner, had been murdered. Seeking solitude, Jesus and His disciples withdrew from the multitudes to the other side of the Sea of Galilee. However, the crowds saw Him leave and they ran around the lake ahead of Him, and were waiting for Him when His boat touched land (Matthew 14:13).

Filled with compassion, Jesus spent the day teaching and ministering to them. That evening, the disciples came and asked Jesus to send the people away into the villages so they might obtain food. He answered and said unto them, "... Give ye them to eat. And they say unto Him, Shall we go and buy two hundred pennyworth of bread, and give them to eat?" (Mark 6:37). A penny was a day's wages for a working man (Matthew 20:1-2). Evidently, the crowd that had gathered was huge.

Jesus commanded the disciples to have the men sit down on the abundant green grass in companies of fifties and hundreds. After He looked up and gave thanks, He began to break the five loaves and two fishes, and filled the baskets of the disciples, who then distributed the food to the hungry multitude. Everyone ate, and everyone was filled, and what's more, everyone saw the miracle. Twelve baskets of leftover food were gathered, more in quantity than the original five loaves and two fishes. The people were so moved by the miracle that they proclaimed Jesus as the Messiah, and tried to forcefully make Him king (John 6:15).

The Bread of Life

At this point, the Lord was at the height of His popularity and renown. He was known the length and breadth of Israel and beyond. Thousands of people flocked to see and hear Him. However, all of that is about to change.

Driven by their stomachs, the crowd followed Jesus and found Him the next day in Capernaum in the synagogue (John 6:26). Their amazement at His presence across the lake was turned to anger at His audacity, as He declared to them that He was the bread of eternal life – that without His flesh and blood, they would have no life in them. The people murmured, even some of His disciples said. "… Is not this Jesus, the son of Joseph, whose father and mother we know? …" (John 6:42). The doctrinal diet was too much for them. They thought they knew Him too well to accept Him as so much. The scripture records that "From that time many of His disciples went back, and walked no more with Him" (John 6:66). From this pinnacle of popularity, Jesus now descended all the way to the utter loneliness of the cross.

There are perhaps those of you reading this who say to yourselves, "I will not do as others have done. I will never leave the Savior." Others have said that, and they have left. What can we do to ensure we are not among those who desert Him – leave Him when the fire gets the hottest?

Remember that Jesus said, "I am that bread of life" (John 6:48). Notice that the Master did not say, "I am the coat of life." He said bread. Bread is the staff of life. It's the mainstay of our diet. It is strength; it is energy; it is life. We do not put it on when we need it. We take it into us continually, and it becomes a part of us. So should His words, His commandments, and His example be what we live on until He becomes us. If you would endure to the very end, take Him in, all of Him, and all the way – no half measures.

The Gentile Woman

SYRIA — *Scriptures: Mark 7, Matthew 15*

Late in the Savior's ministry, hatred against Him had risen to the point where the Jews were trying to kill Him (John 7:1). Rejected by His own, He left Israel and went north into Syria among the gentiles.

Tired and seeking seclusion, He entered a city where a woman identified Him and cried after Him, "… Have mercy on me, O Lord, thou Son of David; my daughter is grievously vexed with a devil" (Matthew 15:22).

The gospel writers point out something interesting about this woman. She was a Canaanite by birth, a Greek by language and custom, and a Syro-Phonecian by nationality. In other words, she was a pure gentile and not at all of the blood of Israel.

Knowing this, how did the Master react to her? He ignored her and kept walking. With faith and persistence, she followed and continued to plead for a miracle on behalf of her daughter. After a time, the disciples became somewhat impatient or annoyed with the woman's pleadings. After all, Jesus had granted miracles to gentiles in the past. Why not now?

"… Send her away;" they said to him, "for she crieth after us" (Matthew 15:23). In other words, "Lord, give her what she wants and get rid of her."

"But He answered and said [to them], I am not sent but unto the lost sheep of the house of Israel" (Matthew 15:24). His mortal ministry was to be among the covenant children of Abraham, and later, through the Holy Ghost, among the gentiles.

The woman then came directly to the Savior and fell before Him saying, "… Lord, help me" (Matthew 15:25).

His answer to her is most intriguing. "… It is not meet," He said, "to take the children's bread, and cast it to dogs" (Mark 7:27). Such an answer may seem harsh that He refers to her as a dog, but when the Savior used the term dogs, a better translation would be little dogs or pet dogs.

It is as though the Savior is saying to this gentile woman, "I am the bread of life. The Father has sent me to feed the chosen people of Abraham's lineage. Now is their time to feast, but your time will come."

The woman immediately caught His meaning, and to her eternal credit she was not offended, but responded, "… Yes, Lord: yet the dogs under the table eat of the children's crumbs" (Mark 7:28).

So impressed was the Lord with this woman's faith that He commended her and granted her request. "… be it unto thee," He says, "even as thou wilt…" (Matthew 15:28).

The woman returned home to find her daughter delivered and lying on her bed.

Some of us may actually feel as unworthy as a dog in the presence of the Lord. Yet, he has perfect compassion, and mercy so abundant and tender that it still cannot be denied, for you and even for the lowest of us who will repent.

THEY WERE OFFENDED

CAPERNAUM *Scriptures: Matthew 15*

The Savior was kind, and filled with charity. Yet there were times when He could be daunting, and very straight-spoken — for example:

The Pharisees and the scribes sought him out, and happened to observe His disciples eating bread without first washing their hands. That bothered them. They took occasion to criticize what they deemed sinful behavior.

According to their traditions, if someone ate without first washing their food and/or washing their hands, they were considered unclean before the Lord. That's how they saw it.

Jesus did not beg pardon, nor did He rationalize the behavior of the disciples. He came right back at them and said to them, "…Well hath Esaias prophesied of you hypocrites, as it is written, This people honoureth me with their lips, but their heart is far from me. Howbeit in vain do they worship me, teaching for doctrines the commandments of men" (Mark 7:6-7).

The Master then went on to cite examples of how the Pharisees themselves set aside the word of the Lord in favor of the word of rabbis. In many instances, their strict adherence to customs and traditions brought them into conflict with the commandments of God, and all too often, Jesus pointed out, God lost.

Then, calling to the multitudes watching this exchange, he announced, "Not that which goeth into the mouth defileth a man; but that which cometh out of the mouth, this defileth a man" (Matthew 15:11).

In other words, it's not what we eat that makes us filthy before God, but what we say, what we think, and what we do. From there, He turned and went into the house. As He did so, His disciples came to him and said, "…Knowest thou that the Pharisees were offended, after they heard this saying?" (Matthew 15:12).

Oh, dear! The Savior hurt someone's feelings! What will He do now? Jesus replied, "Let them alone: they be blind leaders of the blind. And if the blind lead the blind, both shall fall into the ditch" (Matthew 15:14).

Jesus was not about to apologize for wounding their pride. They deserved it. Moreover, He did not want his disciples blindly following them to hell. So, He would let them be offended!

Some have struggled with this story. But please remember, Jesus was and is just and merciful. To be merciful means to be kind and forgiving, treating others better than they deserve. In balance, Jesus was also just. He did only those things that pleased God, and God first!

If we would be true disciples, mercy cannot rob justice, nor can kindness rob courage.

The Deaf Man by Galilee

SEA OF GALILEE   *Scriptures: Mark 7*

Somewhere on an unknown mountain near the Sea of Galilee, Jesus came and sat down and "great multitudes came unto him," bringing with them the lame, the blind, the dumb, and many others similarly afflicted. They came with faith, bringing those they loved and placed them before Jesus – and he healed them. We can only imagine the outpouring of love, gratitude, and spiritual power on that day.

Among the many that were taught and blessed, Mark makes a point to talk about one man in particular who was brought to him. The man was deaf and had a speech impediment. His loved ones asked that Jesus lay His hands on him as well. But rather than bless him before the multitude as He had the others, Jesus instead, drew this man aside away from the crowd. When they were alone, Jesus looked into the man's eyes, put His fingers into his ears and then spit and touched the man's tongue. Then, with the man watching, Jesus looked up to heaven and commanded, "...Be opened" (Mark 7:34). Instantly, the man's "...ears were opened and the string of his tongue was loosed, and he spake plain" (Mark 7:35).

The people were astonished beyond measure at the miracles of the day and glorified the God of Israel. It was truly a day of God's power. But of all the miracles of the day, perhaps healing the deaf man was the greatest. Why did Jesus draw him aside? Why did he put his fingers into his ears? Why did he spit and touch the man's tongue? It was because faith precedes the miracle and this man needed faith. With the man's undivided attention, Jesus put his fingers into his ears to communicate that he was going to remove the obstruction. Then, by spitting and touching the man's tongue he communicated by signs that he was going to heal the man's impediment of speech. It worked. The man's faith and hope were awakened and the power of heaven came down upon him.

Jesus is the author and finisher of our faith. When we have faith already, He can take us where we are and work miracles for us and with us. However, when our faith is nil, He writes it on our heart from the first word, and then labors with us, finishing our faith, until our story is one of peace, power, and perfection.

Upon This Rock

Scriptures: Matthew 16

Caesarea Philippi was a gentile city to the north of Israel and a center of pagan worship. At the time of Jesus, it was associated with the worship of the deities of Baal and the Greek God, Pan. Greeks, Romans, Syrians and other cultures all worshiped here. It was built up by Herod the Great's son, Phillip, the tetrarch of Galilee, and named for the Roman Caesar.

Nearby, a large and powerful spring issued forth from a large cave that became one of the main feeder streams of the Jordan. In addition, the city was built against the backdrop of huge limestone cliffs, into which were carved niches in which the numerous Gods were placed. The large cave would have had a white marble temple placed over its mouth and was believed to be the entrance to the underworld. It was considered a holy place and believed to be a place of revelation and of judgment, where people were thrown into the violent waters to determine their guilt. It is said that the waters of Pan ran continually red with the blood of humans and animals. Moreover, the religious rites that were practiced there would have shocked the sensibilities of Jews and Christians alike.

By design, Jesus departed Galilee and went into the coasts of Caesarea Philippi to be alone in prayer with his disciples. As they walked, Jesus said to them, "...Whom do men say that I, the Son of Man am? And they said, Some say that thou art John the Baptist: some, Elias; and others Jeremias, or one prophets. He saith unto them, But whom say ye that I am?

And Simon Peter answered and said, Thou art the Christ, the Son of the Living God" (Matthew 16:13-16).

While we cannot say with certainty where Jesus was standing when he answered, if he was standing near the Cave of Pan or Banias, as it is called today, then His response is most meaningful and illustrative.

"And Jesus answered and said unto him, Blessed art thou Simon Bar Jona: for flesh and blood hath not revealed it unto thee, but my Father which is in heaven. And I say also unto thee, That thou art Peter, and upon this rock I will build my church: and the gates of hell shall not prevail against it. And I will give unto thee the keys of the kingdom of heaven: and whatsoever thou shalt bind on earth shall be bound in heaven: and whatsoever thou shalt loose on earth shall be loosed in heaven" (Matthew 16:17-19).

Peter, the man of rock, made his emotional declaration that Jesus was the Son of the Living God in the presence and before the faces of a multitude of dead gods – idols of Baal.

As the Apostles looked on at the imposing limestone cliffs before which the worshipers practiced their vain rites, or even beyond at Mount Hermon, the highest mountain for 500 miles, Jesus declared that Peter had received the precious gift of revelation – God had spoken to him, and it was upon that Rock – the Rock of revelation from the Living God, that the Savior's Church would be built.

The gates of hell would not prevail against this rock. The Savior's small group may have been standing before what the pagan world believed were the very gates of hell, over which men had no power. In that physical context, Jesus taught that with the power and gift of revelation, men are born again through the atonement of Jesus Christ, and hell cannot win. Hell cannot claim them in the end. Moreover, Peter was promised the keys of the kingdom of heaven by which he could open and shut heaven and hell through the ordinances and authority of the temple.

It was as though the Savior brought them a two-day journey out of Israel, at the foot of the highest mountain in all the land, to teach by demonstration the eternal and awesome power they were about to receive.

LORD, I BELIEVE

 MOUNT OF TRANSFIGURATION *Scriptures: Matthew 17, Mark 9, Luke 9*

While the Savior was on the Mount of Transfiguration with Peter, James, and John, his other apostles were in the valley below waiting for Him. A man who had a son possessed by an evil spirit came seeking the Master. Since the Master was not present, the disciples attempted to cast out the foul spirit, but because of their lack of faith, they failed. When Jesus came on the scene, He asked that the son be brought to Him, whereupon the evil spirit in the young man threw him to the ground, where he wallowed, foamed at the mouth, and thrashed.

The Master asked the father how long he had been like this. The father replied, "since he was a child." "And many times," he told him, "the evil spirit has tried to destroy him." Then, pitifully, the father pleads, "but if thou canst do anything, have compassion on us and help us" (Mark 9:22).

Now did this man have faith? Yes, enough to come and ask for help, but it's obvious from what he said, not enough to believe that he warranted a miracle.

The Savior, discerning the man's heart and need, said, "... If thou canst believe, all things are possible to him that believeth"Mark 9:23).

Immediately the father cried out with desperate tears in what I consider to be the prayer of the ages. It is as though he spoke for all of us when he said, "...Lord, I believe, help thou mine unbelief" (Mark 9:24).

This father was saying, "Lord, I need thy help. I have no place left to go. I have faith you can help me, but it's not enough to save my son. Please give me more faith to receive thy power."

The Savior answered that prayer, healed the man's son, and restored him whole to his father. I can vividly imagine the father's rejoicing and relief.

It is no different now. Is there any prayer a loving Father would be more inclined to hear and answer than that of a desperate pleading parent? He will hear, and in His own time and way, He will help.

Parents, we don't need to go this alone, not the raising of our children. In this world today, we can't afford to. I want you to know that God has not relinquished His Fatherhood just because He's granted us custodial care. His love for them – our children, and His ability to help them is greater than ours. I believe most of the time He's on our side. It has been aptly said that "one cannot raise Heaven's child without Heaven's help."

37

THE CHASTENING OF THE LORD

 CAESAREA PHILIPPI   *Scriptures: Matthew 14, 16, John 18, Hebrews 12*

It has been said that "… whom the Lord loveth he chasteneth …" (Hebrews 12:6).

To chasten in the scriptures means to correct by punishment, or to inflict pain to reclaim.

It is a true principle that if the Lord loves you, at some point or another, He will chasten you, and it can be very painful and difficult to bear. The question is: Will we bear it? There are some who have not.

In the New Testament, I don't know anyone whom the Lord rebuked and corrected more often than Peter. Remember that stormy night when Peter walked on the water to Jesus? He went out some distance from the boat, his faith failed and fear took over, and he went down like a rock. Jesus saved him, and then said, reprovingly, "…O thou of little faith, wherefore didst thou doubt?" (Matthew 14:31).

Surely Jesus understood why Peter had doubted. So why did He chide him? He had tried, hadn't he? It was because the Lord knew that Peter was better than his performance. Do you know what I find amazing? There's no record in the scripture of Peter pouting or murmuring. He learned and he went on.

At Caesarea Philippi, Jesus announced to His disciples openly that He was going back to Jerusalem where He would "…suffer many things of the elders and chief priests and scribes, and be killed…" (Matthew 16:21). This saying offended Peter. He was upset. He took the Lord "…and began to rebuke him, saying, Be it far from thee Lord: this shall not be unto thee" (Matthew 16:22).

Peter meant well, but evidently innocent intentions do not excuse arrogant attitudes. The Lord turned his back on Peter abruptly, and said, "…Get thee behind me, Satan: thou art an offense unto me…" (Matthew 16:23).

That was harsh! But who was Peter to presume to correct or direct his Lord in His divinely appointed mission? Another rough edge was knocked off of the 'man of rock.'

Remember when Judas came forward in the Garden of Gethsemane with the mob to arrest the Savior? It was Peter who bolted forward with a sword in the Master's defense. Again, he was sharply rebuked. "…Put up thy sword into the sheath: the cup which my Father hath given me, shall I not drink it?" (John 18:11).

Why does the Lord rebuke Peter for trying to defend Him? It is because Peter's actions served Lucifer and not God. Just because we're going hard in service doesn't mean we're going in the right direction. Zeal without knowledge is dangerous!

Compare Peter to Judas. The betrayer was rebuked only once that we have a record of. He was so offended as a result that he sold the Master for his wounded pride. Peter, on the other hand, bore the indignation of the Lord, the shame of His rebuke, the sidelong looks perhaps from his peers, the rumors behind his back, and the slurs on his name even to this day. He bore it all to be with his Lord. Peter is great – not because he was perfect, but because he endured the Lord's discipline to become so.

The Lord changed Peter's name, precisely because Simon Bar-Jona endured and would endure the Lord's chastening. Today he is Peter – the 'Man of Rock.'

Chastening hurts; it hurts a lot! It's "...grievous...", Paul said (Hebrews 12:11). If it is endured though, it disciplines and trains our souls in righteousness. It sweetens our relationship with our Father in Heaven.

It is essential that we understand and believe that a loving Father and Master will never chasten us more than He has the power to heal – but He will chasten!

38

CLOTHED WITH GLORY

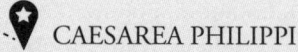 **CAESAREA PHILIPPI**　　　　　*Scriptures: Mark 8*

Easter means that Jesus rose from His tomb immortal. No man had ever done that. The gates of hell had no claim on Him. No man had ever lived like that. The Master rose from His grave, free and unencumbered, determined from that point forward to bring all of us who would come to the same resurrection as His. Our resurrection is our gateway into eternity, but not all resurrections are the same. If we want a resurrection like His, there's something we have to understand.

Jesus traveled far to the north beyond Galilee, near the headwaters of the Jordan River. He had hinted at – but now openly explained to His disciples that He must "...suffer many things of the elders and chief priests and scribes, and be killed, and be raised again the third day" (Matthew 16:21).

This announcement, understandably, startled and upset the disciples. "... Peter took him, and began to rebuke him, saying, Be it far from thee, Lord: this shall not be done unto thee" (Matthew 16:22).

Peter's response was meant in love, but it was out of line.

"...Get thee behind me, Satan:" Jesus said with intense emotion, "Thou art an offense unto me: ..." (Matthew 16:23).

Can you imagine the disciples' shock? Why was Jesus offended? It was because Peter was trying to turn the Savior off-course – away from that glorious moment when, by His resurrection, He was with the Father again. Understanding their bewilderment, Jesus didn't leave them wondering. He gathered them up close, and explained what it meant to be His disciple.

"...Whosoever will come after me," He said, "let him deny himself, and take up his cross, and follow me" (Mark 8:34).

He commanded them further to deny themselves of all ungodliness and lust, and keep the commandments at all costs. They were to forsake the world, and not be ashamed of Christ. If they gave their lives to Him and for Him, they would come up with Him, and be clothed with His glory in the cloud on the right hand of the Son of Man (Mark 8:38).

Then, as if to assure them that such was possible, He added that there were those present who would live to see that day.

For the moment, those disciples could not see the distant good for the looming bad. They were then like so many of us now.

Jesus, on the other hand, was fixed on a glorious resurrection. Does it matter that He had to suffer, sacrifice, and die to obtain it?

So it must be with us. So what if life is unfair, even painful? So what if God, family, and country demand more of us than we think we can give? So what if it hurts? If it brings us at long last to rise with Him, and look at Him as He looks at us, and know Him as He knows us, it will all be worth it.

The pathway to the resurrection and heaven we want may not be what we have expected, but it is certainly the most joyful journey.

39

PATIENCE

 SAMARIA   *Scriptures: Luke 9*

The autumn Feast of Tabernacles was at hand for the Jews. Jesus left Galilee and journeyed to Jerusalem through Samaria. Evidently, somewhere towards evening in their travels they approached a certain village. Jesus sent some disciples ahead to arrange lodgings for the night. But when the Samaritans realized that Jesus, a Jew, was just passing through on His way to Jerusalem, they were offended, and they refused Him their hospitality. It was a deliberate snub to the Son of God. The messengers returned to the Savior and informed Him of the rudeness. James and John were standing close behind the Savior, and they heard the report – and they were upset!

"..Lord," they said, "wilt thou that we command fire to come down from heaven, and consume them, even as Elias did?" (Luke 9:54).

They were upset! Jesus turned and rebuked them saying, "Ye know not what manner of spirit ye are of. For the Son of man is not come to destroy men's lives, but to save them…" (Luke 9:55-56).

With that, Jesus let it go, and moved on to another village.

But what "spirit" were James and John of? It was the spirit of impatience, indignation, and the desire to hurt – or in other words, the spirit of evil. James and John, the sons of thunder, were thundering evil at that moment and they didn't even know it. Surely they felt that their impatience and indignation were justified, just like we often do. I mean after all, those Samaritans had mistreated the Son of God, their Master! But I ask you, just imagine where we'd be if God was as short on patience as we often are? Most of us would have been broiled long ago.

Patience is the quietness and confidence of the soul that yields strength. Patience is part and parcel of faith. Patience is commanded most often in the scriptures in affliction. There is no such thing as long-suffering without patience. It qualifies us to serve the Lord, and is a hallmark of the Lord's people. Finally, patience perfects us.

On that day, John the Beloved wanted to destroy those ignorant Samaritans. But as time went on, he would learn from the Master, and later that same John would give new meaning to the term "long-suffering" as he lived and labored to bring a different fire and light to the children of God.

Lastly, and this is most important. As important as it is to be patient with each other as children of the Lord, it is much, much more important to be patient with the Lord as His child. After all, you have a long way to go, and He has a lot to do with you. So, be still, for in patience you may possess your soul; in impatience you will surely throw it away. Peace.

The Master Teacher

JERUSALEM, FEAST OF THE TABERNACLES *Scriptures: John 7, 8, 9*

In the time of Jesus, the Feast of Tabernacles was held in October and was one of the three great feasts that the Lord had commanded the Israelites to celebrate. Jesus delayed going up to the great feast effectively heightening the anticipation and speculation surrounding Him.

"Where is he?" the people murmured among themselves. Somewhere midway through the feast, Jesus came to Jerusalem and the temple. A few days later, on the eighth or the "great day of the feast," Jesus stood on the Temple Mount and cried, "…If any man thirst, let him come unto me and drink" (John 7:37). This was no random declaration, but a precisely timed and measured invitation.

You see, one of the great moments of this feast was a procession of priests and pilgrims who marched each morning down the hill to the Pool of Siloam and fetched pitchers of "Living Water," brought them back up to the Temple, and poured them over the altar amidst cries from the worshippers of, "We beseech thee, O Eternal, save us, we pray."

It was said that if one had not seen this celebration, they did not know joy. For seven days, the worshippers began each day of the feast with this ritual, but on the eighth day, they did not – though the priests and pilgrims did surround the altar and pray for living water from heaven. The water poured over the altar literally symbolized rain, and the pouring out of living water or the Holy Ghost upon them which brought salvation. It was on that day, in that moment, when that heavenly water that quenches all thirst was not figuratively poured out, that Jesus stood and proclaimed himself the source of all living water to quench all men's thirst. There could be no doubt in all who heard who Jesus claimed to be.

Early the next morning, Jesus was in the Court of the Women on the Temple Mount when He declared, "I am the light of the world: he that followeth me shall not walk in darkness but shall have the light of life" (John 8:12). Once again, this was a calculated declaration both in time and space.

In that very court, as part of the Feast of the Tabernacles, four candelabra were erected, each standing 75 feet high. Each one was topped with four large bowls of olive oil. The number four likely symbolized the giving of light to the four corners of the world. Indeed, when these were lit, it is said there was not a courtyard in Jerusalem that was not illuminated. But on that day, with the Feast concluded and the Temple courts noticeably darker, Jesus declared himself the light of the world.

Just moments later, as proof, He would walk off the Temple Mount, passing a man born blind, and through the elements of living water and light, He brought light to the eyes of a man who had never known it.

Not only was Jesus the Master Teacher, but He was and is the Messiah who will heal us everlastingly!

41

THE ADULTEROUS WOMAN

📍 THE TEMPLE IN JERUSALEM   *Scriptures: Matthew 11, John 8*

How does God really feel about us? We are weak and fallen creatures, prone to make mistakes. It seems to be a part of our fallen nature to be ungrateful and forgetful of all that He's done for us. So with all of this, what are His feelings towards us, His unworthy children? There are many stories of the love of God, but there is one in particular that strikes a resonating chord with many of us.

It was early in the morning. The Savior had come to the temple to teach. A small group had gathered to listen to Him, when suddenly they were interrupted by a commotion. A group of men, Scribes and Pharisees, approached the Savior, dragging a woman in obvious distress. They placed her in the midst of this small group, and with a certain arrogance declared,

"… Master, this woman was taken in adultery, in the very act. Now Moses in the law commanded us, that such should be stoned: but, what sayest thou?" (John 8:4-5).

It was a trap – an ugly, ill-conceived trap. If He said "stone her," he would incur the wrath of the Romans who rule Jerusalem, and He would also be contradicting His own teachings about forgiveness, love, and a higher law. On the other hand, if He said, "release her, let her go," He would appear to be contradicting Moses, the revered lawgiver of Israel, and He would incur the wrath of the people.
The accusation they were leveling against the woman was insensitive and illegal. They had no right nor authority under Moses' Law to do as they did. But in their mind, who cares?

They had Him. There was no way for Him to get out of this one.

For a moment, step back and consider this woman. There is evidently no doubt of what she had done. But did she deserve this? I can imagine her broken in spirit, disheveled, and weeping at the public humiliation she is being forced to endure by evil men.

To the astonishment of the onlookers, Jesus didn't answer. He simply stooped down, and began writing on the ground as though He hadn't heard them. In so doing, He drew all attention away from the woman to Him. They gathered around Him and pressed for an answer. Finally, He raised Himself up and said,

"… He that is without sin among you, let him first cast a stone at her" (John 8:7).

His meaning was crystal clear. He that was without this same sin, adultery, among you, go ahead and stone her. Convicted by their own guilty consciences, each slunk off, leaving only the woman. Jesus raised Himself up again, and seeing none but the woman, he asked,

"… Woman, where are those thine accusers? hath no man condemned thee? … No man, Lord," she said (John 8:10-11).

I love His answer. "… Neither do I condemn thee: go, and sin no more" (John 8:11).

At this awesome display of love and kindness, did that woman then go on to become one of His disciples and follow Him to the end? Surely!

It is a principle of the highest priority in our faith to know that God loves us perfectly, that our weaknesses and our mistakes when we are trying to obey do not anger Him. He knows our mortal condition and has compassion for those who try. His anger is reserved for the rebellious. Our weaknesses and fallen mortal foibles draw forth His grace and mercy. I promise you, no matter who you are or what you have done, you are not beyond the boundaries of His love.

Remember what He said, "Come unto me, all ye that labour and are heavy laden, and I will give you rest" (Matthew 11:28).

42

The Man Born Blind

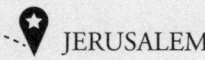 JERUSALEM

Scriptures: Isaiah 8, Matt. 5, John 8, 9

The world is darkening ever more grossly! Modern mass communication serves more to confuse the masses than connect them. This story is for those who hunger and thirst after light and truth.

In the autumn of the year, the Jews held the great Feast of Tabernacles. At the end of the first day of the Feast, the Jews would light the wicks of four huge candelabra. Each candelabra stood 75 feet in height. Once lit, the light given off would light all of Jerusalem. It was during the feast and at the foot of those great structures that Jesus declared, "I am the light of the world."

This declaration sparked a confrontation with the Pharisees that ended in them taking up stones to kill Him.

Following this, as Jesus left the temple precincts, he passed by a man blind from birth. The disciples asked him why this man was blind, and Jesus responded that he was not blind by any fault of his own or his parents, "...but that the works of God should be made manifest in him" (John 9:3). In other words, this man was born blind to be the recipient of a miracle.

Curiously, Jesus then spat on the ground and made clay. He anointed the man's eyes with the clay and told him to go to the Pool of Siloam and wash. Siloam is similar to the Old Testament name Shilo, which is another name for the Messiah. Siloam's waters were considered pure and holy to the Jews.

The blind man obediently made his way down the mountain through the City of David to the Pool of Siloam. He washed and was made whole. He returned able to see. This caused a great stir among the Jews. Everyone knew he was the blind beggar – that he was blind from birth, and now he was whole – but how?

The Pharisees brought him in for questioning. They were presented with a terrible dilemma. Jesus had violated their rules regarding the Sabbath, so obviously, He must be a sinner. But the man born blind was whole. How could a sinner do such a miracle that their law declared could only have come from God?

Jesus could not be of God, for if He were, then they were not. The lowly beggar was summoned before the mighty Sanhedrin, the wisest men of the Jews. With great courage, he defended his healer before them, but they railed on him saying, "...Thou art His disciple, but we are Moses' disciples. We know that God spake unto Moses: as for this fellow, we know not from whence He is" (John 9:28-29).

The absurdity of it all was too much for the restored beggar. He said in effect, "Why this marvelous thing? You are God's holy men and here we have a miracle that your law clearly declares is of God, and you don't know where the man comes from who did it?" With grit in his soul, he declared, "If this man were not of God, he could do nothing" (John 9:33).

The Pharisees could not answer that. His reasoning was irrefutable, so they insulted him and excommunicated him. Jesus found him and further enlightened His soul. "...Dost thou believe on the Son of God?" Jesus asked? (John 9:35). The healed man said, "...Who is he, Lord, that I might believe on Him?" (John 9:36), and then, in one of those rare moments of openness, Jesus said, "...Thou hast both seen Him, and it is He that talketh with thee" (John 9:37). Can you imagine the light and power of witness that flooded his soul at those words? "And he said, Lord, I believe. And he worshiped Him" (John 9:38).

"For judgment I am come into the world," Jesus then taught, "that they which see not might see; and that they which see might be made blind" (John 9:39). Jesus had brought light into a blind man's eyes, and in so doing, enlightened every Jewish soul who knew the blind man. He had effectively declared an undeniable witness before all Israel that He was the Messiah. The sun had risen again over the darkened and benighted world of the Jews. If now they could not see the Son for what He was, it was because they chose to be blind.

Today, the Sun is ablaze again with noonday intensity. Great and marvelous things are happening before our very eyes and greater are to follow. If we choose to believe, we will be flooded with light, within and without, that will ultimately culminate in being transfigured by that very light that will consume the world, but lift us to meet Him. Do we love the light?

Martha And Mary

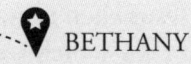 BETHANY *Scriptures: Luke 10*

Have you ever noticed that there is a wonderful dynamic tension in this world of ours? – and tension is the right word. It's good for us to be busy and under pressure to measure up, but at the same time, we're at high risk when we do so feeling overwhelmed and under-qualified. Maybe you know the feeling. Happy and busy is wonderful; miserable and depressed is not. I guess it's like there's this path of perfect balance leading to exaltation, and the goal of life is not to be pulled off either side. So, how do we do this? How do we do all that's asked of us each day without losing the joy that makes it all worth doing? Maybe this story from the life of the Savior will provide an answer.

During the Savior's ministry, He and His disciples entered the small village of Bethany, just south of Jerusalem. The Master went to the home of his close friends, Martha and Mary. Immediately, Martha set to work preparing to feed her distinguished guest, but Mary stayed close to the Savior, sitting at His feet and listening to Him teach. After a time, the burden of the work became too much for Martha. A little put out and impatient, she came to the Savior and said to Him, "… Lord, dost thou not care that my sister hath left me to serve alone? Bid her therefore that she help me" (Luke 10:40). In other words, it sounds like she's saying, "Lord, don't you care that she's left me to do all the work? Tell her to get up and help me."

Tenderly, the Master replied, "…Martha, Martha, thou art careful and troubled about many things: But one thing is needful: and Mary hath chosen that good part, which shall not be taken away from her" (Luke 10:41-42).

Please notice that He never said that what Martha was doing was bad, only that what Mary was doing was better – more important at the time. There are good things, better things, and best things. He is the best of things to give our time to.

Most of us are like Martha. Our time and concerns are taken with the busy work of life, and in a sense that's the way the Lord intended it. But, note this. It is critical that we make the time every day to sit at the Master's feet, as Mary did, and be taught. Those moments of time we spend with Him, praying and in the scriptures, at the feet of the Savior, strengthen our relationship with Him and with our Father in Heaven. By quantity that amount of time may be small, but by quality it makes all the rest of life worth living.

THE GOOD SAMARITAN

 ROAD TO JERICHO *Scriptures: Luke 10*

I believe personally that one of the most difficult things the disciples of Christ will ever be called upon to do in this life is to learn to love, as this story illustrates.

One day, a lawyer stood, and asked a question to Jesus, attempting to put the Master to the test.

"…Master," he said, "what shall I do to inherit eternal life?" (Luke 10:25).

"…What is written in the law," Jesus said, "how readest thou?" (Luke 10:26).

The lawyer quoted the scriptures magnificently. "…Thou shalt love the Lord thy God with all thy heart, and with all thy soul, and with all thy strength, and with all thy mind; and thy neighbor as thyself" (Luke 10:27).

The Savior then said, "…Thou hast answered right: this do and thou shalt live" (Luke 10:28).

Love is the very key to eternal life. Its importance cannot be overstated. Those who will not love cannot be saved.

The Jews believed that only other Jews, however, were neighbors. All others could be justifiably hated. Therefore, this lawyer, in order not to appear a fool in front of the crowd, then followed up with this question: "…And who is my neighbor?" (Luke 10:29).

The parable that followed is called the parable of the Good Samaritan.

The Good Samaritan

A man happened to have a terrible misfortune on the road, and by chance a Priest and a Levite both came upon him in his unfortunate circumstances. God had nothing to do with this occurrence; it just happened. Evil people do terrible things sometimes.

Furthermore, God didn't send the Priest and the Levite down that road. That happened, according to the parable, "…by chance…" (Luke 10:31). They passed the wounded man on the other side of the road, pretending not to see him. When the Samaritan came down the road, and he saw the stricken man, he had compassion and went to him. The message is that love does not ignore a need. It is mercy, compassion, and action.

The Samaritan loaded the man on his own beast, thus making himself walk, and brought the wounded man to an inn and "…took care of him" (Luke 10:34). Love serves and sacrifices. It gives of itself. Not once in this story, or ever in the Lord's teachings about love, does He define the word by what we say. He defines love by what we do!

"If ye love me," – He doesn't say 'tell me,' – He says, "keep my commandments" (John 14:15).

The next day, as the Samaritan prepared to go on with his journey, he charged the innkeeper, "…Take care of him; and whatsoever thou spendest more, when I come again, I will repay thee" (Luke 10:35). Like that Samaritan, life may require us to move on after we see a need, but our love can always remain.

When Jesus concluded the parable, He asked the Lawyer, "Which now of these three thinkest thou was neighbor unto him that fell among the thieves?" (Luke 10:36) – the Priest, the Levite, or the Samaritan?

The lawyer answered and said, "...He that shewed mercy on him" (Luke 10:37).

The Master's reply said it all, "...Go, and do thou likewise" (Luke 10:37).

I find it interesting that the lawyer wanted to know who was his neighbor, and was taught instead how to be a neighbor. Every man we chance to encounter is our neighbor, and an opportunity to draw closer to Heaven. We love them, not by what we say, but by what we do, and by helping them, we save ourselves. Love is not a mortal nicety, my friend; it is an eternal necessity.

45

The Prodigal's Hope

Scriptures: Luke 15

On one occasion, a mixed crowd of publicans and sinners drew near to hear Jesus teach. The Pharisees condemned him for keeping such company. In response, Jesus taught three parables, the Lost Sheep, the Lost Coin, and the Prodigal Son – each one vividly portraying the "…joy that shall be in heaven over one sinner that repenteth…" (Luke 15:7).

It is the parable of the Prodigal Son that captures my hope. The Prodigal Son did not wander off as might a distracted sheep, nor was he lost because of another's carelessness, as in the coin. No, he rebelled against his father – took his inheritance and ran as far away as he could get, where he "…wasted his substance with riotous living" (Luke 15:13). His were some of the most egregious sins.

Then after humiliation, suffering, and extreme want, "…he came to himself…" and said, "How many hired servants of my father's have bread enough and to spare, and I perish with hunger! I will arise and go to my Father, and will say unto him, Father, I have sinned against heaven and before thee, and am no more worthy to be called thy son: make me as one of thy hired servants" (Luke 15:17-19).

At that moment, hope was born anew in his soul, and he set out on the journey home, hopeful, humble, and repentant at last. The scripture says, "And he arose and came to his father. But when he was yet a great way off, his father saw him, and had compassion, and ran and fell on his neck, and kissed him" (Luke 15:20).

I have hope that God still has room in His heart for more than just one prodigal. I hope that He is still standing at the horizon looking afar off, anxious and waiting for me and those I love to come into view. I hope and I yearn for that moment when His welcome will be with those arms of tender mercy that sweep away all sin, fear, doubt, and despair forever.

In this parable, Jesus told me what He and His Father are like – I hope it is true – not that hope that is weak, wishful thinking, but rather that hope which is a lively power that gives me something to live for.

46

LESSONS FROM LAZARUS

 **BPEREA**   *Scriptures: Luke 16*

Have you ever felt that it has been too long since you've heard the voice of the Lord and that you've been too far away for too long? Well, if that's the case, I hope this story is a comfort.

It must have been an interesting day in Perea. As was often the case, Jesus was teaching a mixed audience. His disciples listened and reverenced what He said, while the Pharisees were skeptical and challenged Him. Nonetheless, on that day, Jesus shared a series of parables; ones we're familiar with – the lost sheep, the lost coin, and the Prodigal son.

Perhaps it is because the word 'prodigal' means wasteful that the Lord followed immediately with another parable that's not often mentioned: the parable of 'the unjust steward' – same day, same place. In that parable, Jesus taught the disciples to be wise and prepare for their future, to manage the goods and the means of this world to their benefit and salvation – don't be wasteful or foolish. When He finished that parable, "…the Pharisees, who were covetous…derided him" (Luke 16:14).

That prompted another parable from Jesus. He went on and told the story of a man who had it all. He was very wealthy in the things of this world, dressed in purple, and living comfortably. Outside the rich man's gate there was a beggar, a pitiable creature named Lazarus, full of sores that the dogs came and licked. All Lazarus wanted was crumbs from the rich man's table, and they were denied.

As it happened in the parable, Lazarus died and was taken to heaven. The rich man also died, but he was left in hell. The rich man looked up and saw the beggar, Lazarus, with Father Abraham.

"...Father Abraham," he cried, "...send Lazarus, that he may dip the tip of his finger in water, and cool my tongue; for I am tormented in this flame" (Luke 16:24).

Father Abraham denied the request. "...Son," he said, "remember that thou in thy lifetime receivedst thy good things, and likewise Lazarus evil things: but now he is comforted, and thou art tormented" (Luke 16:25).

The meaning seems pretty clear. God gave the wealth, and the rich man should have shared it. His selfishness damned him. That seems to be a pretty clear message to us as well.

The rich man, seeing that he could get no relief for himself, had his thoughts turned to his family.

"...I pray thee, therefore, father, that thou wouldest send him to my father's house: For I have five brethren; that he may testify unto them, lest they also come into this place of torment" (Luke 16:27-28).

That seems like a logical, reasonable request. If his brothers still living were visited by an angel, surely they would believe and repent. But Father Abraham said "no," and this is my point.

"...They have Moses and the prophets;" he said, "let them hear them" (Luke 16:29). He's talking about the scriptures. The rich man said "...Nay, father Abraham: but if one went unto them from the dead, they will repent" (Luke 16:30).

This was Father Abraham's reply, "...If they hear not Moses and the prophets, neither will they be persuaded, though one rose from the dead" (Luke 16:31).

Lessons from Lazarus

The scriptures talk to us. They are more powerful and persuasive than the presence of angels. It has been said, and I believe it, that if you want to talk to God, pray. If you want God to talk to you, study the scriptures.

By the way, it turns out Jesus was right. He was always right. Within just days, the Savior's friend Lazarus did die and did come back from the dead, just as they had asked – and as He had predicted, they didn't believe.

47

That One Leper

SAMARIA *Scriptures: Luke 17*

I don't know how it works, but to "count your many blessings" and "name them one by one" not only promotes a spirit of gratitude, but it also fosters a spirit of humility. That's why I've always appreciated Thanksgiving. It's that one season of the year when we all stop and give thanks for what we've received.

One day while Jesus was passing through a village, He was met by ten men afflicted by leprosy. From afar off they pleaded for His healing mercy. Interestingly enough, He did not approach them and they did not approach Him, as He had done in times past. He simply said, "...Go, shew yourselves to the priests..." (Luke 17:14).

Let me mention something about leprosy. Leprosy was a dread disease. It was literally a living death, mostly incurable. The afflicted not only rotted and died one painful degree at a time, but the torment was added to by banishment from family, friends, and civilized society. The only companion that a leper could have were other lepers. There could hardly be a more miserable way to live or die.

At the Savior's command, the ten journeyed towards the priest to be judged. As they went, they were miraculously healed! Nine of them, Jews, continued on where Jesus had sent them, but one of them turned around, and ran all the way back to the Savior, and fell on his face before the Lord giving Him heartfelt thanks. The man was a Samaritan, and not even of Jesus' race or religion.

That One Leper

In a way, you and I are like those lepers – spiritually. We come into a wicked, fallen world and, through no fault of our own, contract spiritual diseases that leave us, if left untreated, sick, suffering, lonely, and destined to die. There is One to whom our pitiful appeals from afar do not go unheeded. Mercifully, the Savior speaks and sends us on our way, and as we journey toward our judgment, we too are healed from a living death. We live again; we are given a new life.

Like that Samaritan, take the time to turn back, fall before Him, and with a heart full of thanks, remember all that He has done for you. It is well to keep in mind that there were ten lepers healed. Only one, the most lost of all, turned back to say, "Thank you." Do not be of the nine – let us be the one.

The Importunate Widow

GALILEE Scriptures: Luke 18

Do not ever give up on God, especially in prayer.

Jesus once spoke in a parable of an importunate widow. The word "importunate" means that she was persistent to the point of being annoying in asking for help. It seems that someone had unjustly wronged this woman, and with no other recourse, she went to the law for justice.

However, the judge that heard her case "… feared not God, neither regarded man:" (Luke 18:2).

He was a hard, cold man, who at first turned a deaf ear to the needy widow. Evidently, she continued to come and ask for help until she became an annoyance to the judge.

Finally – and there seems to be some exasperation – he said, "… because this woman troubleth me, I will avenge her, lest by her continual coming she weary me" (Luke 18:5).

The Savior then said to His disciples, "… Hear what the unjust judge sayeth" (Luke 18:6).

It seems as though the Lord is assuring His disciples in this parable that if a cruel-hearted judge will help those who continue to ask, even more surely will God, who is just and compassionate, help His children. God is the opposite of that unjust judge. He is just. He is compassionate. Rather than this being a parable of similarity, this is a parable of contrast. God will answer the prayers of His faithful children. When our cause is just, and it's important that it is, we are commanded to persist in prayer.

The Importunate Widow

We "... ought always to pray," the scriptures say, "and not to faint;" (Luke 18:1).

Why does God require us to ask over and over again? Why doesn't He just give us what we want the first time we ask? I don't know. But this much I do know: I know what my children really want by how often they ask, and how willing they are to work for it.

When God does not grant our endless prayers for what we need so badly, there's a tendency to believe that He's like that unjust judge, that He too seems not to regard us. When we've asked over and over, and no answer has come, we may say in our hearts, "If He knew how much this hurt, and how much I really need Him, He would help me."

This parable is meant to assure us that He does hear, and He will make all things just, and fair and right, even though it may take a long time!

I know of few things in this life that are a more wrenching test of faith than unanswered prayers. Therefore, the critical question upon which our faith rests is this: When God will not do what we want, when we want, will we still love Him and do what He wants?

49

Obedience Always

PEREA *Scriptures: Matthew 19, Mark 10*

What is the purpose of life? Of the many things that you have to get done today, which is the most important? To every Christian that is now or ought to be, this story reveals the answer.

One day, while Jesus was on the road, a young man came running after Him. Upon reaching the Master, the man knelt at His feet and asked, "...Good Master, what good thing shall I do that I may have eternal life?" (Matthew 19:16).

Jesus responded to Him the same as He had earlier done with the lawyer. He referred him to the scriptures. "Keep the commandments," He said (Matthew 19:17). "...Do not commit adultery, Do not kill, Do not steal, Do not bear false witness, Defraud not, Honour thy father and mother" (Mark 10:19). Whereupon the man said, "...Master, all these things have I kept from my youth up; what lack I yet?" (Matthew 19:20).

How many of us, like this man, have gone charging after the Lord, filled with zeal and momentary enthusiasm, only to wander away later when something else caught our attention? I cannot recall how many times I have prayed with all my heart for help and answers and then paid little attention when those answers came.

May it be understood that it is one thing to come unto the Lord, but it is another to follow Him thereafter. Any man who asks the Lord for revelation had better be prepared to obey it when it comes, or he is worse off than if he had never asked.

Jesus loved the rich young ruler, and, out of respect for his agency, gave Him what he asked for. He wanted a great thing revealed, and it was.

"One thing thou lackest:" the Savior said, "go thy way, sell whatsoever thou hast, and give to the poor, and thou shalt have treasure in heaven: and come, take up the cross, and follow me" (Mark 10:21).

The young man "...was sad at that saying, and went away grieved; for he had great possessions" (Mark 10:22).

I wish this story was a parable, but it is not. It is history that I fear continually repeats itself. Obedience is the first law of heaven, and the foremost duty of man. It is the sum of our existence, and the only source of our joy is to find the truth and obey it.

What then is the most important thing you can do today? Find out exactly what the Lord wants and obey the same way.

The Pharisee and the Publican

PEREA   *Scriptures: Luke 18*

I want to tell you a story, which is true, but never actually happened. It's a parable told by the Savior about two men praying in the temple.

One of the men was devoutly religious. He worked with great diligence to be strictly obedient to all of the commandments of God. He was greatly respected and admired by the people around him. So faithful was he that he paid a larger tithe than was asked and fasted twice a week – far more than was required.

The other man seemed to have been somewhat dishonest in the past. He was despised and dishonored, even outright rejected by his fellows. By some he was considered to be a traitor to his country. There even seemed to be evidence that he cared little for God and His commandments, up until now.

Which of these men would you guess was standing favored with the Lord? Surprisingly, it was the second man. Why? It has been said that out of the abundance of the heart the mouth speaketh. Listen to these fellows as they pray.

The first man, a Pharisee, a religious leader among the Jews, prayed as follows:

"… God, I thank thee, that I am not as the other men are, extortioners, unjust, adulterers, or even as this publican. I fast twice in the week, I give tithes of all that I possess" (Luke 18:11-12).

He sounded quite smug and sure of himself.

Now hear the prayer offered by the second man, a publican, which was kind of like an ancient version of the Internal Revenue Service. He was a tax collector. He felt so unworthy that he beat on his chest, he wouldn't lift his eyes or even stand near the devout Pharisee. He prayed simply,

"...God be merciful to me a sinner" (Luke 18:13).

To the publican's prayer the Lord responded, "I tell you, this man (meaning the publican) went down to his house justified rather than the other ..." (Luke 18:14).

This man, the publican, was a model for us all, because no matter what his past had been, his present was humble and repentant – not arrogant, nor self-righteous. Thus, he was right with God, and at any cost, that's what we want to be.

51

Bartimaeus

 JERICHO   *Scriptures: Mark 10*

To those who are prisoners, those who are caught and bound by circumstances not of their choosing, there is a man in the Bible you should meet. His name is Bartimaeus.

On the Savior's final journey to Jerusalem, He passed through Jericho. As He came out of the city with a large group of people, He passed by a man sitting, almost like litter, on the side of the road. It was the blind beggar, Bartimaeus.

Bartimaeus heard the commotion and asked what was happening. When he learned that Jesus of Nazareth passed by, hope surged within this man like a shock, and suddenly he became animated and cried out with a loud voice, "…Jesus, thou Son of David, have mercy on me" (Mark 10:47).

Those with Jesus rebuked Bartimaeus, and told him to hold his peace. Why did they want to silence him rather than to help him?

Bartimaeus would not be deterred. He only cried the louder. To his fellows, Bartimaeus was an irritation and an interruption, but to Jesus, he was like a crying child. The Savior stopped and commanded him to be brought. Now, suddenly the rest of them cared. "…Be of good comfort," they said, "rise, He calleth thee" (Mark 10:49).

Bartimaeus then did something interesting. The scriptures say he threw off his garment and went to Jesus with excitement. Why does it matter to Mark, the gospel writer, that he threw off his garment? It's because this was the mark and depth of Bartimaeus' faith.

Have you ever paid attention to the clothing a beggar wears? It's not usually a fashion statement. The garment, like the man, would not be the latest craze, but rather cast off, tattered, and forgotten. For Bartimaeus to cast off his old garment was the same as casting off his old life. He was no longer going to need it.

With earned compassion, the Master asked him, "…What wilt thou that I should do unto thee?" (Mark 10:51).

Somehow word of this healer had reached Bartimaeus before Jesus got there. From those windborne seeds of rumor, faith blossomed, nurtured by the pain of his personal bondage. Blindness was Bartimaeus' prison and sight would mean a new life.

"…Lord," he pleaded, "that I might receive my sight" (Mark 10:51).

"…Go thy way;" Jesus said to him, as He touched his eyes, "thy faith hath made thee whole…" (Mark 10:52).

Bartimaeus was healed. Now, free at last to see and to go his own way, Bartimaeus followed in the Master's way. What way was that? It was the ascending road from Jericho to Jerusalem, where the mists of darkness had so blinded the minds and hardened the hearts of its citizens that the Light of the World, Jesus, would die on Calvary's Hill.

Just as there are none so blind as those who will not see, so too there are none so bound as those who bind themselves. No prison is ever permanent though when there's faith in the Savior.

If you are that prisoner, have you had enough? If so, cry unto Him for mercy. Be patient in pain until it's time, for that pain can purify your soul and prepare your faith. When He visits you, throw off your past like filthy, disgusting clothing.

Remember that agency may have put you in prison, but in Christ and His grace, no prison is permanent.

Bartimaeus, who wore rags, came out of the gutter, set free, that day in Jericho.

52

Mary's Kindness

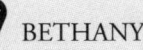 BETHANY

Scriptures: Matthew 26, Mark 14, John 12

Just days before His atoning death, Jesus came to Bethany, where he was hosted for supper by Martha, Mary, and Lazarus. As Martha served the meal, Mary suddenly came to the table, broke open an alabaster box of ointment, anointed the Savior's head and feet, and wiped them with her hair. The house was filled with the sweet-smelling lotion. Some of the disciples began to murmur.

"Why was not this ointment sold for three hundred pence and given to the poor?" Judas complained (John 12:5).

Their unkind words must have stung Mary's tender soul.

Jesus came immediately to her defense. "…Let her alone; why trouble ye her? She hath wrought a good work on me…. she has come aforehand to anoint my body to the burying" (Mark 14:6-8). Then he added these solemn words, "…Wheresoever this gospel shall be preached in the whole world, there shall also this, that this woman hath done, be told for a memorial of her" (Matthew 26:13).

What a promise! Jesus wanted this woman to be remembered for all time by every disciple who ever remembered Him. Why? What was it in that simple deed which was so important to Him?

First, that ointment was not your ordinary lotion. It was spikenard from India, and worth almost a year's wages for a working man. It was an uncommon, sacrificial offering. Next, to anoint one's head and feet, as she did Him, was an act of reverential homage, rarely rendered even to kings.

Further, she had saved the ointment for His burial, thus indicating that where so many of His disciples did not believe His ominous predictions of death – she did! Even the perfect Son of God was so affected by her timely kindness that He memorialized her for all time.

Every measure of cruelty and unkindness we give to another will be remembered and returned to us when the Lord comes again. If we do not repent, we will have to face and then feel all the hurt we have brought on others. Those who have practiced the godly art of kindness will bask in the warmth of the Savior's loving tenderness on that day. To be kind to others is to be kind to Him.

The Cleansing

 JERUSALEM *Scriptures: Matthew 24*

Near the end of the Savior's ministry, two significant events occurred which warrant discussion.

On the last Monday of the Lord's life, He entered the temple in Jerusalem and found in its courts a scene that angered Him. Flocks of cattle and sheep were milling and bawling. Moneychangers with their tables exchanged current coinage for temple coinage that pilgrims might pay the temple tax. Haggling vendors sold their wares in a scene which would remind us of a carnival. The noise, the stench, and especially the blasphemous desecration of holy ground moved the Lord to indignant anger. With whip and thunderous command, He drove them out into the streets where they belonged. No one dared oppose Him, not even the leaders of the Jews whose pockets were being lined by ill-gotten gains. Why? It was because in guilt there is weakness.

Twice the Lord cleansed the temple – once at the beginning of His ministry, and again at the end. I have pondered this and wondered if there's a broader parallel. The Lord "cleaned house" once on this earth with a flood. The second time it will be with fire – and clean it will be; of that we may be assured.

The second story takes place the following day, on Tuesday. While in the precincts of the temple, He prophesied the total destruction of the temple, and denounced the leaders of the Jews for their hypocrisy and corruption. Upon leaving the temple, He retired to the solitude of the Mount of Olives. As He sat, probably looking over the city, His disciples came to Him privately and asked Him when the temple would be destroyed. They wanted to know when the prophecy would be fulfilled and what the signs of His second coming would be. The Savior's answers to those questions constitute Matthew 24, in the discourse on "the signs of the times."

My purpose here is not to enumerate those signs, but to look carefully at the emotional aftermath they had on the disciples. He described to the Twelve such horrible things as wars and rumors of wars, the whole earth in commotion, and men's hearts failing them for fear just before His coming. He spoke of the love of men in our day, waxing cold, and iniquity abounding. He told of earthquakes, desolating sicknesses, and men killing one another. When He finished, the Apostles were visibly scared and upset. Jesus calmed them by saying, "…be not troubled, for all these things come to pass…" (Matthew 24:6).

If the original Twelve Apostles were troubled by those signs of the times, most of which would not even occur in their lifetime, how much more understandable it is that we in whose day they are being fulfilled should be troubled. Yet, there is no need to let either the signs, or the flood of wickedness and corruption around us unduly concern us. The Good Shepherd is right on schedule, and He has not abandoned the flock just because of a little bad weather and some ravening wolves among us. I quote Him again, "Be not troubled" (Matthew 24:6).

54

HYPOCRITES

 THE TEMPLE MOUNT *Scriptures: Matthew 23*

There are those who have created an image of a Savior who is so gentle that He's never angry; so kind that He's never harsh; so forgiving that He winks at sin. Such an image is dangerously wrong and can foster a casual attitude toward the Lord's commandments.

The reality is that Jesus cleared the Temple with a whip, rebuked Peter and turned His back on Him, and renounced and insulted the Pharisees publicly. Matthew 23 always seemed so out of character to me – until I paid more attention. You'll remember that the Master's foremost accusation against the Pharisees was hypocrisy. Why was He so scathing on that subject? As this is a sin that worries many who are trying to be good, perhaps it's needful to understand what it is, and why the Savior felt so strongly about it.

Hypocrites – all the world hates a hypocrite. A hypocrite is a pretender and a deceiver. The word itself is Greek in origin and means actor. Generally, it is someone who espouses a cause and publicly professes allegiance to certain standards, while secretly living a double standard. In short, they preach high standards and live low lives. That's a hypocrite.

Some religious people are frequent targets of this accusation, but not all deserve this label. You see, hypocrites are conniving deceivers. They know what they're doing. They deliberately walk in two opposite worlds. This is different from those who are living to the best of their knowledge and ability, who are genuinely trying, but are still beset with weakness. A man cannot be a hypocrite when he continually acknowledges his weakness, and compels no man to live better than he does.

Hypocrisy piggybacks arrogance, since both are an outgrowth of pride run amok. Hypocrisy tends to be judgmental of others – harsh, exacting, and unjust. It may talk compassionately, but it does not act it out. Hypocrisy revels in glory and attention, and devours praise and flattery as greedily as fine food. Hypocrisy is obsessed with its public appearance. It will go to extreme lengths to create an image of virtue, but close proximity always finds the filth within. Hypocrisy tends to be vicious in its efforts to maintain an ill-gotten place. Those who attempt to expose it will be publicly vilified.

Hypocrites are especially dangerous and destructive to the Savior's cause. Why? It is because they slither undetected like vipers among the Lord's people. When they're finally found, they destroy not only the individuals they have deceived, but the entire group becomes characterized by the loathsome behavior of that one person. Hence, not only do hypocrites lead away their friends, but they bring the whole cause into public condemnation, principles and all. Perhaps it is for this reason that the only public vice more loathsome than a hypocrite is a traitor. Traitors are usually quickly discovered and disposed of, while hypocrites can work undetected for years.

Hypocrisy always has victims. Usually they are innocent people and pure principles. Both are ruthlessly sacrificed to feed a hypocrite's ego. This is why the Savior of the world so soundly and publicly renounced them, and will inevitably detect every vestige of hypocrisy in His people and expose it.

Hypocrites

Hence, trying to live your religion and teach it meekly to others – that's exactly what you should do. Judge not the sins of others lest you are found and judged by your own faults. Just do the best you can, and let others do the same.

The Widow's Mite

HEROD'S TEMPLE, JERUSALEM

Scriptures: Mark 12, Luke 21

Jesus stood in the richly furnished courts of the Temple of Herod, and in the midst of heckling opposition denounced the leaders of the nation for their hypocrisy and their selfish wickedness. The Temple, which previously He had called "My House," He now disowned. Moving away from the open court of the Temple, Jesus entered the Court of the Women, where there were thirteen trumpet-shaped chests that comprised the treasury of the Temple. There He sat, downcast and in deep sorrow, and probably wept. Then, looking up, Jesus saw a poor widow, known as such by her clothing of mourning, come forward and cast two mites into the treasury. A mite had the smallest value in their monetary system and compared to our money today would be worth less than half a cent.

Immediately, discerning the heart of the situation, Jesus called His disciples to Him, and pointed out the deed of the woman, declaring, "…Verily I say unto you, That this poor widow hath cast more in than all they which have cast into the treasury: For all they did cast in of their abundance; but she of her want did cast in all that she had, even all her living" (Mark 12:43-44).

It is no accident that Jesus drew attention to this simple deed during this critical time at the end of His public ministry. A walking object lesson, this woman taught the selfish wealthy in simplistic ways among individuals and nations, that it is not the size of the offering that counts as much as the heart and the sacrifice behind it.

What about us? Is there someone we should visit? Is there a letter we should write, or an offering that we should make that we haven't? Let's follow the example of this woman.

56

HAPPY ARE YE

THE UPPER ROOM OF THE LAST SUPPER *Scriptures: John 13*

Are you happy? I mean really – are you happy? Even more importantly, do you know how to be? I don't think I have ever met a person who didn't want to be happier. The problem is, I'm not sure too many people know how. As far as I know, the Savior only mentioned happiness once in the New Testament, but in that story there is a great key – a key to happiness. If you don't mind, I would like to share it with you.

It was the last night of the Savior's life. Ironically, it was that same night of the dark and depressing spirit that led Him to Gethsemane.

He and the Twelve Apostles were gathered in the Upper Chamber to partake of the Passover meal. During the course of the meal, the Savior rose unexpectedly from the table, removed His outer garments, wrapped a towel around His waist, and after the manner of a common household slave, and with a basin of water and a towel, bowed to wash the dusty feet of the Apostles. He came to Peter. Peter realized what the Savior was about to do, and protested, "Thou shalt never wash my feet!"

Peter must have felt it beneath the Savior's dignity to perform such a lowly and menial service. But the Savior explained to him, "If I wash thee not, thou hast no part with me" (John 13:8). At that point, Jesus moved around the table washing the dusty feet of each apostle with careful concern for significant details.

He came to Judas, that offended, murderous, and conspiring apostle, knowing full well what was in his heart, and yet the

Savior with equal love and tenderness removed Judas' sandals – and washed the dirt of Bethany's road from his feet.

When the Master finished, He then taught the Apostles that they too should follow His example, and humble themselves, even as He had done, and be a servant – not a master – a servant for those they were to lead, and perhaps especially for their enemies. Then He gave them this significant promise saying, "If ye know these things, happy are ye if ye do them" (John 13:17).

Consider what He is saying as coupled with what He has done. In other words, to serve is to be happy. It would not be material possessions that brought happiness to the apostles. They left all of that behind. It would not be looking out for their own lives that was going to bring them happiness. They gave their lives to look out for the Lord's sheep. In short, by giving up what the world said would bring happiness, peace, and power, they gained all three – and they gained it forever.

If we would be happy, we should go and serve all humanity as He did.

57

BE OF GOOD CHEER

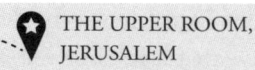 THE UPPER ROOM, JERUSALEM   *Scriptures: John 16*

Have you ever found yourself saying, 'I'll be happy when…" – or, "Life will be good as soon as…" Well, from a very old and familiar story, I gained some insights into this. Life doesn't work that way.

Remember that last night of the Savior's life? It was a wrenching, emotional experience for the disciples. An already difficult night was made unbearable by the things He was telling them. To their shock and dismay, He announced that one of them would betray Him. The sacramental cup that followed was the token of a tearful farewell. The disciples were filled with sorrow.

To add further to their distress, He assured them that all of them would be offended because of him that very night and would abandon Him. Peter was aghast. He denied he would ever do such a thing, and when he did, the Savior prophesied Peter's denial.

Jesus continued and assured them He was going away. He wouldn't leave them comfortless though. Then in earnest, as Gethsemane was only moments away, Jesus said to them, "If the world hate you, ye know that it hated me before it hated you" (John 15:18). "…the time cometh," he continued, "that whosoever killeth you will think that He doeth God service" (John 16:2).

He also said, "…ye shall weep and lament, but the world shall rejoice: and ye shall be sorrowful, but your sorrow shall be turned into joy" (John 16:20).

Be of Good Cheer

Finally, He stated, "Behold, the hour cometh, yea, is now come, that ye shall be scattered, every man to his own, and shall leave me alone…" (John 16:32).

Look carefully at the Savior's final words to His Apostles in this life. There's a quality of earnestness about them, almost an urgency that pulls on the heartstrings. He desperately wanted them to understand what was ahead of them. The forthcoming days of their ministry were going to be very hard! Their faith would be tried nearly unto death. The people they were commanded to love would hate them, revile them, and finally kill them!

How could this be? These were the Lord's chosen servants. Of all people that should be respected, it should have been them. Of all people that life should have gone well for, it should have been them! Jesus repeatedly warned them to be prepared.

Then, after telling them all these hard things that were going to happen, He said, "These things I have spoken unto you, that in me ye might have peace. In the world ye shall have tribulation: but be of good cheer; I have overcome the world" (John 16:33).

There it is! It was as though Jesus was saying to them, "Your life is going to be hard; expect it, embrace it; find your joy and peace in the heat of trial and don't wait for the end of it!" Joy is found in the midst of the difficulty, not when it's over!

If you think about it, life really is only as hard as we believe it is. If we're looking for trouble, we'll find it aplenty. If we're looking for peace and joy, we'll find it in Christ abundantly.

THE ANNUNCIATION

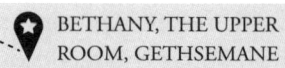

BETHANY, THE UPPER ROOM, GETHSEMANE

Scriptures: Matthew 26, John 12, 13, 17

Of all men in all of human history, one man is perhaps the most infamous, at least in the Judeo-Christian world. He is a traitor, a murderer, even a devil incarnate (John 6:70). His name has come to be an epitaph for a traitor of the worst stripe. Who is he? – one of the twelve apostles, Judas Iscariot. It would have been better for this man never to have been born (Matthew 26:24). Have you ever wondered what happened that took this man from being one of the Lord's to what Jesus called a "son of perdition"? (John 17:12).

Judas Iscariot is reported to have been the only man of the Lord's Twelve Apostles who was not a Galilean. He was from Judea. After spending all night in prayer, Jesus chose from among His disciples twelve who would be his apostles, one of them being Judas. Why he was chosen, we just don't know, nor do we have that much personal detail on him in the gospel record. What we do know is he was evidently the treasurer for the Twelve, keeping and disbursing funds on their behalf, and he had an inordinate love of money, such that John labeled him a thief (John 12:6).

One evening, at the home of Martha and Mary in Bethany, Jesus sat down to supper. Mary came into the room with an alabaster box of very valuable ointment, and anointed the Lord's head and feet. It was an act of profound love, respect, and humility. Judas, however, filled with indignation, protested and said, "Why was not this ointment sold for 300 pence and [the money] given to the poor?" (John 12:5). His brutish insensitivity drew forth the Lord's stern rebuke. "Let her alone:" he said, "against the day of my burying hath she kept this" (John 12:7).

It wasn't long after this event that Judas gave himself to a different master. The scriptures record, "...Satan entered into him..." (John 13:27). Knowing that the chief priests and the Pharisees wanted Jesus dead, essentially putting out a contract on Him, Judas went to them and said, "...What will ye give me and I will deliver him unto you?..." (Matthew 26:15). It was the money thing again. Delighted with that arrangement, the chief priests promised to give him thirty pieces of silver, and from that point forward, Judas looked for an opportunity to betray Jesus into the hands of the Pharisees.

Later on at the Last Supper, Jesus washed the feet of the Twelve, including Judas. Then sometime during the course of that meal, He excused Judas to fulfill his murderous intent. "...That thou doest," Jesus said, "do quickly" (John 13:27). He knew full well what was in Judas' heart.

Judas left the room and went out into the night. He led the chief priests and the soldiers to where Jesus was in the Garden of Gethsemane, and then betrayed Him with a kiss. Because of that betrayal, the Son of God was murdered. Afterwards, for whatever reason, Judas went out and hanged himself, committing suicide. His became a terrible story of eternal tragedy!

Could it have been avoided? Yes. It could. Had Judas not chosen to be offended by the Lord and His words, the tragedy may have been averted.

Heaven help us to understand that if we ever find ourselves offended at the Lord or His servants because of the word, we are on very dangerous ground!

59

LOVE AS JESUS EXPRESSED IT

 THE UPPER ROOM   *Scriptures: Matthew 7, John 13, 14, 16, 21*

Years ago, I ran outside to catch my six-year-old son as he walked to school. I felt something that I did not want to resist. I felt a warmth and an affection that I had to express. I caught up with him, pulled him into my arms tightly and said, "I love you, son." He responded, "I love you too, Dad." I then lifted him to the other side of an icy puddle too wide for him to cross, and he went on his way to school.

What is love? The dictionary defines love as a feeling or affection that we have for someone or something because of some benefit we receive. That kind of love is what the scriptures call the love of men." It is the kind that waxes cold. We hear people say, "I love my family for all that they do for me." What happens when they stop doing, or we do not care for how they are doing it? Love dies, and the object of that love is replaced.

The love of God is different. It is pure, unfailing, and endures forever. I can only imagine how charged with emotion that upper room must have been on the night of the Last Supper. "A new commandment I give unto you," Jesus declared, "That ye love one another; as I have loved you, that ye also love one another. By this shall all men know that ye are my disciples, if ye have love one to another" (John 13:34-35).

This is not a new commandment. It was given to Moses. What is new then? From that day forward, the Lord's disciples were to love with His love, as He loved. The old commandment was, "…all things whatsoever ye would that men should do to you, do ye even so to them…" (Matt.

7:12), but the new commandment was to treat others as Jesus would.

Still, in the quiet of that upper room, Jesus continued, "If ye love me, keep my commandments" (John 14:15). Notice that He did not say, "if ye love me, tell me." The world is full of those who draw near with their lips, but their hearts are cold and distant. God's love is affection expressed with action. "This is my commandment, that ye love one another, as I have loved you" (John 15:12). "Greater love hath no man than this, that a man lay down his life for his friends" (John 15:13).

There it is. The highest expression of love known to God or man is to lay down one's life for another. The most perfect way to say I love you is to do for that person as God would. Perfect love is inspired love. Perfect love always involves sacrifice on the part of the person expressing it.

Within moments of teaching them this doctrine, Jesus put it into expression saying "…that the world may know that I love the Father; and as the Father gave me commandment, even so I do. Arise, let us go hence" (John 14:31). "Hence" was the Garden of Gethsemane and the cross.

They wanted him to stay. They grieved and wept over him. He was breaking their hearts, and He knew it (John 16:6). Jesus also knew that the greatest love He could express now was not what they wanted, but what God wanted for them. The Lord taught and cheered them as well as they could understand. He sealed them up unto the Father by His prayers and faith, and then left them for Gethsemane.

Gethsemane and Golgotha were the greatest expression of love this world has ever known. He poured out His soul unto death. He laid down His life for the Father and for us. He took that life up again and gave it to us forever.

Not all will receive His love. Hardened hearts cannot feel it. Do not judge the presence of God's love by what you do or do not feel, for it is always there. You may destroy your sensitivity to it by disobedience, but you can never kill His affection for you – not now, not ever.

Later, on the shores of the Sea of Galilee, the resurrected Lord asked Peter, "Simon, son of Jonas, lovest thou me? Yea Lord; thou knowest that I love thee," Peter answered.

"Feed my sheep," came the Master's reply (John 21:16). His disciples mattered so much to Him that He gave His best men for them. He still does!

Now you come to God, and he fills you with His love and sends you out to give it away, starting with your family. You love them as you love them because you get to do for them, not because they do for you. This is love.

GETHSEMANE

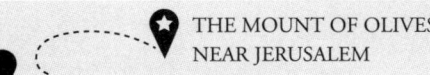

THE MOUNT OF OLIVES, NEAR JERUSALEM

Scriptures: Matthew 26, Mark 14, Luke 22, John 18

A story more important than any other is the Savior's atonement in the Garden of Gethsemane. This is a story that needs to be heard and understood by anyone who has ever wrestled with the bitterness of guilt and the blush of shame, by anyone who has ever felt burdened and inadequate, by anyone who has ever felt worthless and alone, and by anyone who has ever felt that life had no purpose and was not worth living.

After the singing of a hymn, Jesus and the Twelve Apostles left the upper room of the last supper and made their way out of Jerusalem to the Mount of Olives. Taking Peter, James, and John, Jesus entered the solitude of the Garden of Gethsemane, a place where olives were grown and then crushed under intense pressure to extract their life-sustaining oil.

Jesus invited the three apostles to "…tarry…and watch." (Mark 14:34)

He then went about a stone's throw away and collapsed face-first to the ground praying, "…O my Father, if it be possible, let this cup pass from me: nevertheless not as I will, but as thou wilt" (Matthew 26:39).

After some time in prayer, Jesus returned to the three apostles, and interestingly enough, they were asleep. Jesus woke them saying, "…What, could ye not watch with me one hour? Watch and pray that ye enter not into temptation…" (Matthew 26:40-41).

Jesus left them again, and again, in incomprehensible physical and spiritual agony, brought on by the sins of all mankind and the onslaught of all Hell itself, He bowed beneath the load and prayed, "…O my Father, if this cup may not pass away from me, except I drink it, thy will be done" (Matthew 26:42).

Luke records that "…there appeared an angel unto him from heaven, strengthening him. Being in agony, he prayed more earnestly: and his sweat was as it were great drops of blood falling down to the ground" (Luke 22:43-44).

When He returned the third time, the apostles were again asleep. Shortly after, Judas came and betrayed the Master with a kiss. Jesus was then arrested, and with a rope around His neck, was led away eventually to the cross, where His atoning sacrifice was completed.

The Savior took upon Him in that garden the sins, pains, sicknesses, and infirmities of His people. His atonement was an infinite burden of sin and an endless stream of individuals. For that moment in time, He who knew no sin and guilt became for us the greatest sinner of them all. Truly, He is our compassionate high priest that can "…be touched with the feeling of our infirmities" (Hebrews 4:15).

He understands us, and can help us as no one else can.

By virtue of His precious blood, shed from every pore of His body, He stands, by heavenly right, between us and justice, pleading our cause eternally.

The Atonement of Jesus Christ is not a legend of long ago and far away. It is a vital truth, an active principle so intimate and intertwined with our daily existence, that even now we would fall in profound gratitude if we had even a mustard seed of a glimpse. What happened in Gethsemane is infinite in scope and profoundly personal. We were all there in a sense, and those precious drops of blood falling down the ground were for us individually. How many drops of blood were shed for you?

I tell this sacred story because more than anything, I want the hopeless and overwhelmed to have hope. His suffering and sacrifice places us in His power. He can help us. I know how much He can help. Therefore, "Let us…come boldly unto the throne of grace, that we may obtain mercy, and find grace to help in time of need" (Hebrews 4:16).

Turn to Pray

Scriptures: Mark 14, Luke 22

Where did the Savior go immediately after His baptism and just before the ministry that would end with His life?

Answer: He went out into the wilderness to fast and to pray for forty days, in closest communion with His Father. Why?

Where was the Master on the eve of that crucial day when His most trusted friends and associates that would be with Him in His ministry, namely the Twelve Apostles, were to be chosen and ordained?

Answer: The Savior was on a Galilean mountain where He spent the night in prayer with His Father.

Where did the Savior with a troubled heart turn when the multitudes misunderstood Him and tried to make Him a king against His will?

He went to the mountains, and again, He spent the better part of the night in prayer with His Father.

When the missionaries came back, the missionaries that He had sent out – when they returned rejoicing in their great success and the miracles they'd seen, what was the Master's reaction to their rejoicings?

"In that hour Jesus rejoiced in spirit, and said, I thank thee, O Father, Lord of heaven and earth, that thou hast hid these things from the wise and prudent, and hast revealed them unto babes..." (Luke 10:21). Interestingly, He rejoiced in prayer with them.

Lastly, in those monumental moments of Gethsemane, when the fate of all humanity hung in the balance, Jesus was in the deepest agony of any mortal ever known. Where did He turn for strength?

He turned where He always has – to His Father.

"… Abba, Father, all things are possible unto thee; take away this cup from me: nevertheless not what I will, but what thou wilt" (Mark 14:36).

"And being in an agony," Luke records, "He prayed more earnestly: and His sweat was as it were great drops of blood falling down to the ground" (Luke 22:44).

Where do we turn? Where do we turn when we're happy? Where do we turn when we're sad? Where do we turn when we need strength or council? Don't turn to the world. I pray that our relationship with our Heavenly Father will be so close, so constant, and so personal that it is our deepest nature and first impulse to turn to Him, and only Him, in all our moments of need.

The Body and Blood

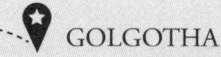 GOLGOTHA　　*Scriptures: Leviticus 17, Isaiah 53, Matthew 26, Luke 22, 1 Peter 2, 1 John 1*

For any and all who have ever pondered the Communion of Christ, please consider this story.

On the last night of the Savior's life, He entered the Garden of Gethsemane with his disciples, all of them being subjected to feelings and emotions exquisitely intense. The record says that Jesus himself "…began to be sorrowful and very heavy" (Matthew 26:37). He was weighed down, even to the point of death (Matthew 26:38). His burden must only have been made worse by the knowledge in His heart that His disciples, His closest friends, were doubting Him and complaining of Him at this crucial hour.

Jesus went from them a short distance. He knelt and fell on His face on the ground saying, "…Abba, Father, all things are possible unto thee; take away this cup from me; nevertheless not my will, but what thou wilt" (Mark 14:36).

What's happening to Jesus? Clearly, this moment in Gethsemane is much more than a heartfelt prayer. Whatever "this cup" is that Jesus mentioned, He had been preparing for it from the very beginning. Whatever it was, it had crushed Him to the earth, and brought Him to the point of death. It was so terrible that "…there appeared an angel unto him from heaven, strengthening him" (Luke 22:43).

Then Luke recorded one of the most meaningful verses in all of sacred writings, "And being in an agony he prayed more earnestly: and his sweat was it were great drops of blood falling down to the ground" (Luke 22:44).

The Body and Blood

The Lord's body was racked with agony such that great drops of His blood were forced from every pore of His body. Isaiah had spoken of this moment when "…He hath borne our griefs and carried our sorrows:…" (Isaiah 53:4).

Since the beginning of time, God had commanded his children to sacrifice animals as a type and shadow of this moment – a prefiguring. He had decreed that "…the life of the flesh is in the blood: and I have given it to you upon the altar to make an atonement for your souls: for it is the blood that maketh an atonement for the soul" (Leviticus 17:11).

Since that time, the children of Israel had taken their animals, placed their sins upon them, and then shed the animals' blood upon the ground as an atonement, worshiping Christ, the real Lamb of God, as they did so. That would have been the ancient version of Communion.

In His body, Christ did what no Paschal lamb could ever do. Our sins were not only placed on Him, but they passed through Him as well. The sacrificial lambs never felt the anguish that Christ did. Here, and at the Cross, Jesus "…bare our sins in his own body…" (1 Peter 2:24).

Hence, we are asked to remember that body. It was the sacred instrument of the atonement allowing Him to "…justify many; for he shall bear their iniquities" (Isaiah 53:11).

Christ's blood was His life. To take His blood was to take the life of a God – and that was the atonement. That precious blood that dripped upon the ground that night was payment for our sins. As John said, "…the blood of Jesus Christ his Son cleanseth us from all sin" (1 John 1:7).

Anciently, the saints worshiped and pondered the meaning as a lamb died before them. The bread and wine of the sacrament are sacred. By them, we have communion with Him and a remission of our sins through them.

63

Pain

GETHSEMANE AND GOLGOTHA

Scriptures: Isaiah 53, Matthew 26

In Gethsemane, the Lord Jesus suffered pain of body and spirit in totality. It caused Him to sweat blood and shrink, but He saw it through. Then Judas, a friend, betrayed Him with a kiss. Peter grabbed his sword and rushed to defend the Savior. But the Savior stopped him saying, "Thinkest thou that I cannot now pray to my Father, and he shall presently give me more than twelve legions of angels?" (Matthew 26:53).

Jesus knew the suffering ahead of Him, and yet not only did He go willingly to the scourging and the cross, He wouldn't allow anyone to take it from Him. Roman soldiers led Jesus up Golgotha's hill to crucify Him. Crucifixion was torture! It was agony!

Before they nailed Him to the cross, they offered Him a drink of vinegar mingled with gall, and when He had tasted the vinegar, He wouldn't drink. Gall was a drug that was intended to deaden the pain. Why did the Savior refuse it? It was because He wanted the pain. He had to have it, all of it – all of ours, for all of us.

Jesus was crucified for the sins of the world. The cross was part of His atonement by which He paid for our sins and redeemed us. His suffering was essential to an infinite atonement.

There is pain of the body, and there is pain of the spirit. It is our nature as mortals that when we hurt, we want it to go away. The healthcare industry is a testament to the price we are willing to pay for remedies to our pain.

Pain

Pain can be healed, avoided, or ignored. Jesus did none of these. His incomprehensible pain had purpose, and He invited it, and as a perfect man, He would feel everything perfectly; nothing diminished His anguish. Moreover, the Father gave Jesus a greater measure of pain for His mortal sojourn than any other person has ever borne, and Jesus bore it meekly.

Isaiah used the word "bear" deliberately when he said, "Surely he hath borne our griefs and carried our sorrows…" (Isaiah 53:4). "…By his knowledge shall my righteous servant justify many; for he shall bear their iniquities…(Isaiah 53:11), and "…he bare the sin of many…" (Isaiah 53:12).

Oh, it is wonderful what He bore! I stand all amazed that He stood it. By His pain I live; by my own pain I learn.

Praise be to God for pain, and for you that are in pain – patience. It will pass in His Time.

64

PONTIUS PILATE

JERUSALEM   *Scriptures: Matthew 27, Luke 23, John 19*

When Isaiah spoke of Christ, he said he would "… be for a sanctuary; but for a stone of stumbling and for a rock of offense …" (Isaiah 8:14). Jesus later added, "… whosoever shall fall on this stone shall be broken: but on whomsoever it shall fall, it will grind him to powder" (Matthew 21:44). It would seem that the most important mortal decision we will ever make is how we respond to the Savior and how soon.

Jesus was arrested in the Garden of Gethsemane and brought to the palace of Caiaphas, where he was illegally tried and condemned. Early the following morning, Jesus was bound and led to the judgment hall, where he stood before Pontius Pilate, the Roman governor (John 18:28; Mark 15:1).

Why was He there? It's because the Jews did not have the authority to put Jesus to death. That power belonged to Rome (John 18:31). Moreover, if the chief priests and elders put Jesus to death, there would be a hue and cry across Jerusalem. If the Romans condemned him, there was little the people could do, and it would seemingly justify the decision of the Jewish Sanhedrin. Therefore, Pilate became the pawn in the plot to kill the Messiah.

Who was Pilate, and how did he come to be in this unenviable predicament? Tradition holds that he was born and reared in central Italy, a Roman citizen. He was the political appointee as prefect of Judea under the Roman Emperor, Tiberius, in 26 CE. While Pilate maintained his headquarters in the coastal city of Caesarea Maritima on the Mediterranean coast, he came with soldiers to Jerusalem, to the Antonia Fortress, to maintain order during the great feast days.

It was here that Jesus and Pilate met. Pilate immediately recognized there was "… no fault in this man touching those things whereof ye accuse him" (Luke 23:14). No less than eight times did Pilate attempt to release Jesus, but the Jews would not have it. They insisted that he die. Even after being warned by his wife to "… Have thou nothing to do with that just man…" (Matthew 27:19), Pilate finally gave consent for the Savior's death and washed his hands of the matter (Matthew 27:24).

Pilate was afraid of Jesus (John 19:7-8), but he was more afraid of Rome and the people. It was judicial murder and Pilate knew it.

Pontius Pilate mostly disappeared from the biblical record after those eventful days. Yet the few existing secular records indicate that in 36 CE, Pilate was summoned to Rome before the emperor, Caligula, to answer charges of excessive cruelty. He was subsequently deposed, disgraced, and ordered by the Emperor into exile, where Pilate would take his own life.

We do not know for certain what happened to Pilate, but this much is known: his name has sunk into infamy along with Judas Iscariot and Herod.

The choices we make about Jesus the Christ are the most important and far-reaching decisions we will ever make now and forever.

Watch the Lamb

Scriptures: Revelation 5

The Apostle John made a statement in the Book of Revelation which said, "...Worthy is the Lamb that was slain..." (Revelation 5:12).

Some two thousand years ago, the Jews of Jesus' day commemorated the Passover, that sacred event from their history when the angel of death passed over them, while all the firstborn among the Egyptians died.

On Thursday, sometime in the late afternoon, Peter and John, at the Savior's command, took a lamb and, under the direction of the priests in the temple, they killed it and spilled its blood. Then they prepared the Passover for Jesus and the rest of the Twelve. That evening, Jesus and the Twelve Apostles came to partake of the last officially authorized Paschal supper.

For four thousand years, God's people had been sacrificing the lambs and shedding their blood as an offering for sin. Even now, thousands of lambs would be killed over those two days.

For years, the thought of such a thing, and especially as part of my religious devotions, seemed distasteful and disgusting. Why would God have commanded such a thing of them?

I don't know all the reasons, but as I have studied it and thought about it, I learned some interesting things. The lamb was a symbol to point them to the time when their Redeemer would come and be the final lamb offering. For example, consider some of the following:

Each of those lambs selected was male, unblemished and perfect, just as Jesus would be.

Each was innocent, undeserving of its fate, just as Jesus would be.

Each was meekly submissive, just as Jesus would be.

Each was brought by the head of the household to be sacrificed on behalf of the family, just as Jesus would be.

Each had its blood forcefully shed and thus its life taken, just as Jesus would.

Each was sacrificed in the holy place, just as Jesus would be in the holy city.

Each Passover lamb was sacrificed under the authority of Israel's priests, just as Jesus would be.

Each was sacrificed without a bone broken, just as Jesus would be.

Each lamb was of the first year, cut off in the bloom of life, just as Jesus would be.

Finally, each had another's sins placed upon it, and vicariously died for them, just as Jesus would.

After the shedding of great drops of atoning blood in the Garden of Gethsemane, Jesus was led away like a lamb to Golgotha, where on Friday morning, He was lifted up and sacrificed. For some six hours, He hung in indescribable agony. Then sometime around 3 o'clock in the afternoon, perhaps even while the Paschal lambs were dying in the temple, Jesus died, the ultimate offering for the sins of the world.

In His offering I have part. Because of it, I can be encircled in the arms of mercy. No more were the lambs to die. It was not necessary. The horrible price was paid. Man was free!

Now, in conclusion, for many years I was tempted to rail and accuse those who missed the significance of the lambs and their blood when it was fulfilled, until it occurred to me that unless and until I understood the significance of the bread and the wine, I had better be quiet.

66

THING OF NAUGHT

 GOLGOTHA

Scriptures: Psalms 59, Isaiah 53, Mark 15, Luke 23

On Friday, the Son of God and Lord of Life was judged as evil and not worthy to live. They stripped Him of His clothes and nailed Him to a Cross. He was crucified for our sins. He died for us.

Have you considered how His atoning agony, already incomprehensible, must surely have been intensified by the cruel words of those who stood by His cross? Look carefully at what they said as He hung and suffered there.

Those passing by "...railed on Him, wagging their heads, and saying, Ah, thou who destroyest the temple, and buildest it in three days, save thyself, and come down from the cross" (Mark 15:29-30).

Can't you just hear the taunt, "If you really were of God and had the power you claimed, you would come down from there?"

The Chief Priests joined in and said, mockingly, "...He saved others; let Him save Himself, if He be the Christ, the chosen of God" (Luke 23:35).

It was as if the rulers were saying to all Israel, "See, He's not of God. God would never let such a thing as this happen to a truly righteous man."

Even the soldiers took up the mocking chorus saying, "...if thou be the King of the Jews, save thyself" (Luke 23:37).

Finally, the thief at His side said, "If thou be Christ, save thyself and us" (Luke 23:39).

All seemed to be saying, "You are a liar. If you were all you said you were, this would not be happening to you. Hypocrite! Deceiver!"

Did all of this hurt the Savior? Oh, yes! Through the Psalmist, He said, "Reproach hath broken my heart; and I am full of heaviness: and I looked for some to take pity, but there was none; and for comforters, but I found none" (Psalms 69:20).

They did not understand. No good man, they assumed, and especially the Son of God, would ever be crucified. They arrogantly judged Him as evil by His circumstance, just as Isaiah said they would.

"Surely He hath borne our griefs and carried our sorrows: yet we did esteem Him stricken, smitten of God, and afflicted" (Isaiah 53:4).

They blindly considered Jesus' crucifixion as punishment by God and so accused Him. What they did not understand was that Jesus the Just was being punished for us, the unjust. His suffering was ours, and His death was for us. God was punishing Him with our stripes, and their caustic words only made it worse.

When it was said, "...they shall look upon me whom they have pierced" (Zechariah 12:10), I wonder, if it was only the spear that pierced His heart that day?

Today, the worst of things will happen to the best of people: rebellion of children, ruin, scandal, and divorce. May it be that never again will we make their heart's cross heavier by our wagging heads and careless words. I have come to believe that those who spend their time weighting the crosses of others will sooner or later get figuratively nailed to one.

67

SERVE THY MOTHER

 CANA *Scriptures: John 2, John 19*

There are only three known references to Jesus' direct interactions with His mother after His public ministry began. These references are very enlightening.

The Savior's ministry had just begun. He returned to Galilee from His baptism at Jordan, and His temptation experience in the Judean wilderness. He came with His disciples to a wedding feast at Cana. It may well have been a member of His family getting married since it was Mary who was in charge of the feast – we really don't know. But during the course of the festivities, they ran out of wine. Mary came to Jesus in her need and said to her son, "They have no wine" (John 2:3).

Did she know that He had the power to work miracles? Of course.

Had He done it before? Of course.

Jesus could have considered the request trivial, and scoffed at it, but He didn't. I love the way Jesus talks to His mother. "Woman," he said, "what have I to do with thee; for mine hour is not yet come" (John 2:4).

Now note this: The use of the term 'woman' was not like we use it today. It was then a title of great respect. Even according to some, in this context, it was a reference to a woman of queenly caliber. It was as though He was saying to her, "Mother, I will do for you whatever you want. Your wish is my command."

That is exactly what the Master did. Miraculously, He created a more than ample supply of the highest quality wine to finish out the feast.

Now, let me take you back. Remember what He said to her? "...Mine hour is not yet come" (John 2:4).

What did He mean by, "[His] hour is not yet come?"

Not surprisingly, it turned out that Jesus' hour was 'Gethsemane and Golgotha.' He was born for that moment of moments when He would suffer and die to save the human family. So in effect, the Savior was saying to His mother, "I can help you now, but not then."

Yet – and this is so significant – when do we find the next major interaction between Jesus and His mother? It came in the midst of His 'hour.' He was hanging on the cross of Calvary, suffering an incomprehensible weight of agony, and from that cross He looked down where His mother stood with John, the beloved disciple. Both were grieving near the cross. Jesus looked at His mother, and with the tenderest of concerns, said to her, referring to John, "Woman, behold thy son" (John 19:26). Then He looked over at John and said, "Behold thy mother!" From that hour, John took her unto his own home" (John 19:27).

With the salvation of worlds innumerable, and of an infinite humanity weighing upon Him, I find it touching – overwhelming, that Jesus still had the time and the concern to see to the temporal salvation of His mother as one of His last acts of kindness before He died.

If only we would all do the same. Surely, it is no accident that Jesus' public ministry began and ended with tender acts of kindness for His mother.

JESUS THE PIONEER

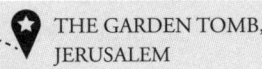

THE GARDEN TOMB, JERUSALEM

Scriptures: Matthew 28, Luke 23, John 20

We remember and honor the great patriots and pioneers of our past. It seems that the more we value what those of the past did for us, the more sacred their memory becomes to us. So in that spirit, if a pioneer is one who at great personal risk and sacrifice made the journey first and opened the way for us to follow after, would you consider who, in my humble opinion, is the greatest pioneer of all history?

Late on Friday afternoon after some six tortuous hours hanging on the cross of Calvary, the Lord Jesus Christ cried with a loud voice these final words, "…Father, into thy hands I commend my spirit…" (Luke 23:46). Having said thus, the Savior of the world died.

Sometime before dawn on Sunday morning, the Lord returned in spirit to His body, and by the power of the Spirit of God, He raised that body from death and re-entered it, never again to be divided. The angel of the Lord descended and rolled back the sealed stone from the Garden Tomb, but Jesus had already left.

As the signs of an impending sunrise became evident, Mary Magdalene and other women came to the tomb . They were greeted by angels who announced, "He is not here: for he is risen…" (Matthew 28:6).

A short time later, that same Mary was back at the tomb, this time alone and grieving. She supposed that someone had stolen the Lord's body. So inconceivable was the rising of someone from the dead, especially one whose body has been so thoroughly destroyed as was the Lord's, that the angel's words, "He is risen", just simply had not registered. The Lord came behind Mary. She saw Him, but did not recognize Him. Supposing that He was the caretaker of that garden where the tomb was, she asked him if he had any knowledge of where the body of the Lord had been taken.

Then, the Lord said, "…Mary…" (John 20:16).

Something about the tone and tenderness by which He spoke her name caused her to recognize Him. She ran to embrace Him. The Lord stopped her, and sent her to tell the disciples what she had seen.

Later that night, ten of the Twelve were gathered together, still skeptical of the many reports of the Lord's rising from the dead. As they were talking, the Master appeared before them. So overwhelmed were they that they could not believe their eyes for joy.

I don't think it was accidental or incidental that in each case of the Lord's personal appearance after His resurrection, there was a dramatic emotional shift from deep pain and doubt to indescribable joy.

Please consider, if a pioneer whose efforts affected the most people, for the greatest good, and for the longest time deserves the greatest adoration, then, the Lord Jesus is the greatest pioneer of them all. Literally, all our hopes, our dreams, our loves and joy for all eternity – our happiness here and hereafter – come because He went first and broke the bands of death.

We may not see or understand it now, but someday I believe we will count His pioneering Atonement and Resurrection as one of the greatest gifts a generous God could ever have given.

Resurrection Morning

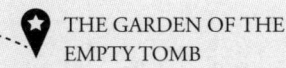

THE GARDEN OF THE EMPTY TOMB

Scriptures: John 20

Mary Magdalene was a most blessed woman, but you should know that before God exalts, He always brings low.

Sunday morning while it was yet dark, Mary came with the other women to complete the anointing of the Lord's body. They found the stone already rolled back, and His body gone. Angels greeted them and instructed them to go and tell His disciples that He was risen, but they did not understand what that meant.

Mary Magdalene ran to tell Peter, while the other women went to tell the disciples. Peter and John received that news, and immediately ran to the tomb to see for themselves – and indeed, He was gone!

The two apostles left the sepulcher and returned to their homes, but Mary stood outside the tomb – weeping, as she had already done for so many hours that weekend. His disappearance now from the tomb was one more devastating blow to a heart already broken beyond belief. She had lost him again! The Jews, out of hate and spite, must have stolen His body, she thought. Weeping, she stooped down and looked once more into the tomb.

Two angels dressed in white asked her, "…Woman, why weepest thou? …" (John 20:13).

Her answer revealed her anguish, "… Because they have taken away my Lord, and I know not where they have laid him" (John 20:13).

At this point, Mary turned around and saw Jesus standing nearby, but didn't recognize Him.

The Savior comprehended her tears and pain, and was moved with compassion for her. "Woman," He said, "… why weepest thou? Whom seekest thou? …" (John 20:15).

She thought He was the gardener with authority for the grounds and pleaded with Him, "… Sir, If thou have borne him hence, tell me where thou hast laid him, and I will take him away" (John 20:15). While saying this, she turned her back to Him and looked once more into the empty tomb.

"… Mary. …" Jesus said. (John 20:16).

Mary turned. She recognized Him, and a torrent of light and joy flooded through her soul – as exquisite as had been her grief for a long weekend.

"… Rabboni; which is to say, Master," she cried (John 20:16).

Overcome with emotion, she ran to Him, desiring to hold Him, and express with her arms what she felt in her heart. She had lost Him once on the cross, and again when she thought His body was stolen. Never, never would she let Him go again!

Understanding her heart, Jesus said to her, "…Touch me not; for I have not yet ascended to my Father …" (John 20:17), or in other words, "Mary, you can't keep me here. I have to leave."

Now to you – all of you who love the Lord, Mary was the first to see Him, but won't be the last. Her reunion with Him revealed something of what it will be like for you who have loved Him, and lived your whole lives proving that love.

You will see Him again – with joy!

70

THE SAINTS WHO AROSE

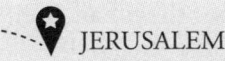 JERUSALEM   *Scriptures: Ezekiel 37, Matthew 27, 1 Corinthians 15*

The resurrection of the Lord Jesus Christ completed His atoning work, and was the greatest event in the history of this world. Those who witnessed His resurrection to immortal flesh and bone numbered in the thousands, and spanned the globe. Of necessity, Christ's resurrection was one of the most well – attested events ever to transpire, and those witnesses continue to this day!

From the days of Father Adam, mortal men were taught that Christ's Atonement would conquer death and open the grave for all men. That valley of dry bones which was seen by Ezekiel (Ezekiel 37:4,11) would indeed come forth in perfected flesh and bone. The resurrection was to be a literal corporeal restoration to life.

As Jesus was called the first fruits of the resurrection in the scriptures, what of the fruit that was to come after? That is a story seldom told and too often overlooked at Easter.

The earthquake which accompanied the Savior's death in Jerusalem rocked the entire world! All across the globe, the graves of the dead were thrown open by it, and the bodies of the saints who were dead came forth – and there were many! In the Holy Land, Matthew recorded that the dead rose "… and went into the holy city [of Jerusalem], and appeared unto many" (Matthew 27:53). Can you imagine what that day must have been like?

Not only there, but what of the faithful who had died in Christ in other parts of the Lord's vineyard? He had other sheep scattered all over the world. Surely, they saw Him as well.

On that first Easter, not only was it witnessed by many that He had risen, but also it was witnessed that others had risen because of Him. The story of His resurrection is sacred. It's central to our faith and doctrine, and hence, that story belongs to all of us, while the stories of those individual saints and their resurrection – well, that's personal, and it belongs to them and their families. We know little about it in detail.

It stands documented and verified by witnesses that Jesus rose and His tomb was empty. It also stands proven that the dead rose because of Him. Christ's resurrection was the promise. The resurrection of those other saints was the proof of His promise. The dead rose, and they will rise again.

"O death where is thy sting? …" (1 Corinthians 15:55). I think of all those stung by death who have lost loved ones, and still miss them. That sting is made easier when we consider they will be resurrected. That sting will be healed forever on the day that He comes – and He will come, and so shall your loved ones who have passed beyond this mortal life.

The Stranger on the Road

 ROAD TO EMMAUS   *Scriptures: Matthew 25, Luke 24*

Just after Peter and John had come at Mary's bidding to the empty Garden Tomb, two disciples left Jerusalem for the village of Emmaus, about 7-8 miles distant. Not only does no one know for certain exactly what village was Emmaus in that country, but little to nothing was known for certainty who these disciples were. Only one was named – Cleopas. It has been suggested that the other disciple was Luke.

As the two men walked, "they communed together and reasoned." A stranger drew near to them and asked "...What manner of communications are these which ye have one to another, as ye walk and are sad? One of them, whose name was Cleopas, answering said unto him, Art thou a stranger in Jerusalem, and hast not known the things which are come to pass there in these days? And he said unto them, What things?..." (Luke 24:17-19).

The two disciples then said, "...Concerning Jesus of Nazareth, which was a prophet mighty in deed and word before God and all the people:" (Luke 24:19). They then told him how the chief priests had condemned Jesus and delivered Him over to be crucified. The disciples revealed the source of their grief and sadness, saying, "But we trusted that it had been He which should have redeemed Israel..." (Luke 24:21). Do you see what they are saying? They were going through a faith crisis. Their faith was shaken, and their hearts were grieved and troubled by rumors of angels, and reports that He was alive. With their mortal understanding, they knew assuredly that He could not be alive.

At that point, the stranger said to them, "...O fools, and slow of heart to believe all that the prophets have spoken: Ought not Christ to have suffered these things, and to enter His glory?" (Luke 24:25-26). The stranger then opened up the scriptures and taught the words of the holy prophets concerning the mission and ministry of the Messiah. As He did, their hearts burned within them and they knew the truth of His words, and the power of that man.

This conversation must have lasted for miles, because about this time they approached the village of Emmaus. It was towards evening, and the stranger made as though to journey on, but the two disciples said, "...Abide with us: for it is toward evening, and the day is far spent..." (Luke 24:29).

The mysterious stranger accepted their gracious invitation for hospitality, lodging, and food. "And it came to pass, as he sat at meat with them, he took bread, and blessed it, and brake, and gave to them. And their eyes were opened, and they knew Him; and He vanished out of their sight" (Luke 24:30-31). It was Jesus, their Lord and Master. He was, indeed, alive. It was Him all along.

This story does attest that a resurrected being can eat and drink, hide his identity, and look like a normal man. This story may mean many things, but to me it means at least this. Cleopas and his companion invited a stranger to abide with them and receive their hospitality, and in so doing, the Lord came to them and gave them so much more than they gave him. Remember when the Lord said, "...Inasmuch as ye have done it unto one of the least of these my brethren, ye have done it unto me" (Matthew 25:40). What if they had turned the stranger away? What if they had just let Him go on his way?

Could it be that each time we literally or figuratively invite a stranger close to abide with us and receive our love, comfort, and kindness, it is He who comes to abide. We are the ones who receive greater comfort and love.

That is an experience we can't wait to tell the whole world about.

72

LOVEST THOU ME

 SEA OF GALILEE   *Scriptures: John 21*

After the Savior's resurrection, He appeared to the Apostles in the Upper Room, manifesting a real, physical, and corporeal body to them. Eight days later, He came similarly to Thomas.

Sometime after those profound events, Simon Peter and four others were at the Sea of Galilee when Peter announced, "…I go a fishing…" and those with him said, "…We also go with thee…" (John 21:3).

They spent the rest of the night fishing in the familiar waters of the Sea of Tiberias. Peter, James, and John had earned their livelihood fishing these waters. It was from those shores years before that Jesus had called them to follow Him and be fishers of men.

Now they were home again, back on the lake, and the mortal ministry of the Messiah was over. Could they have been wondering, "Now what do we do?"

They fished the lake all night and caught nothing. The next morning, a stranger called to them from shore, "…Children, have ye any meat? They answered him, No. And he said unto them, Cast the net on the right side of the ship, and ye shall find…" (John 21:5-6).

They did as the stranger bid them, and immediately their nets were filled with so many fish that they could not draw them in. It was exactly what the Lord had done to them more than three years earlier. At that moment, they recognized Him! It was the Master!

When they got to shore, Jesus had a meal of cooked fish and bread waiting for them.

As they finished eating, Jesus said to Peter, "…Simon, son of Jonas, lovest thou me more than these?…" (John 21:15). What are "these?" Could it be that right here he is holding up or gesturing to the fish?

Peter answered Him, "…Yea, Lord; thou knowest that I love thee…" (John 21:15).

Without preamble, Jesus responded, "…Feed my lambs" (John 21:15).

Then Jesus asked the question again, "…Lovest thou me?…" (John 21:16).

Peter's answer was the same, "…Yea, Lord; thou knowest that I love thee…" (John 21:16).

This time the Lord responded, "…Feed my sheep" (John 21:16).

Then a third time, the Lord asked the same question. The scripture says that Peter was grieved that the same question had been asked of him. Why was the Lord repeatedly asking him a question for which He already knew the answer?

Peter replied,"…Lord," he said, "thou knowest all things; thou knowest that I love thee…" (John 21:17).

Once more came the simple command, "…Feed my sheep" (John 21:17).

The repetition of three made a memory in Peter that he never forgot!

Once before, by a miracle, the Lord had called Simon Peter from his nets. Now similarly, He was calling him away again and back to work by the same miracle – except this time, the work would end in Peter's martyrdom, not the Lord's.

At the same time, Jesus taught Peter and all of us what a disciple's purpose is in this life. Our love for the Lord is measured by our love for others. A man or woman filled with love for God can't rest. They must move; they must love by action. To love Him is to love His children.

There are so many things we can do with our time each day, but of them all, helping His people pleases the Lord the most. He pays the highest dividends of joy to those who invest their time in His sheep.

73

CHANGE

JERUSALEM   *Scriptures: Acts 3, 4*

I am convinced that almost anyone can change. The purpose of life is to change and prepare to meet God. The sacrifice of the Savior insured that choice, and to me no character in the scriptures exemplifies change more than the Apostle Peter.

Three times on the night of the Savior's betrayal, Peter denied Him, even after publicly proclaiming he would never forsake Him. The record says after the third denial, the cock crowed and Peter went out and wept bitterly.

I can only imagine the depth of Peter's pain and guilt at what he had done. Surely it must have been one of the lowest points of his life. I've often wondered what thoughts filled his mind during those three days that Jesus was in the tomb. Could it have been something like this?

"There's no hope for me now. I can never be forgiven. My sin is too great. I've sinned too much. How could He ever love me again?"

If the story of Peter's life had ended there, it would have been a tragedy indeed. But, it didn't. On the day of the resurrection, Peter was privileged with a personal visit from the risen Lord, face to face, one on one. Peter was forgiven, and once more encircled in the arms of the Savior's love. It changed him. The interview was so sacred that nothing of the details was recorded. That change in Peter was dramatically illustrated by an event which occurred about two months later.

Late one afternoon, Peter and John walked into the temple. As they passed through the gate called "Beautiful," a man, crippled from birth, begged alms of them.

"… Look on us," Peter commanded (Acts 3:4).

The man looked at them expecting to receive something of them, but Peter said, "… Silver and gold have I none; but such as I have give I unto thee. In the name of Jesus Christ of Nazareth rise up and walk" (Acts 3:6).

Peter reached down and lifted the man to stand on feet that had never borne weight and the people saw him "…walking, and leaping, and praising God" (Acts 3:8). The healed man entered the Temple rejoicing.

When word got out of Peter preaching to the people and what he had done, he was questioned by the Jews who asked "… By what power, or by what name, have ye done this?" (Acts 4:7).

Boldly, Peter declared, "…by the name of Jesus Christ of Nazareth…doth this man stand here before you whole" (Acts 4:10). Then Peter added this vital truth, "…there is none other name under heaven given among men, whereby we must be saved" (Acts 4:12).

Under the refining hand of the Master, Peter's weakness became the catalyst for his strength. Eventually, he became like the Master he worshiped, a man of miracles, eventually even a martyr.

Peter is a pattern for all those who want to change. Whether we are now in the rock bottom of bitter tears and regret for past mistakes, or simply stranded on a plateau of complacency, when invited, the Savior comes and will encircle us in the arms of His love. The effect is we are changed, and never again the same.

74

SAUL

ROAD TO DAMASCUS   *Scriptures: Acts 9, 26*

In my lifetime, I have met some wonderfully talented people with great abilities in everything from the fine arts to industrial arts. All of these people have made their contribution in one way or another to the human race. But, there is one who has perfected the talent – of humanity; He has perfected people. It is the Lord Jesus Christ. He is mighty to save and cleanse us. There is no one who loves us more, has a greater desire to help us, and more power to do so than He.

Who would have thought in 34 A.D. that Saul of Tarsus would become a Christian? If you read the story, if ever there was a man who was anti-Christ, and an unlikely Christian, it was Saul.

When the devout Christian, Stephen, was stoned by the Jews for his testimony of Jesus, it was Saul who stood by as a witness and consented to the murder.

It was Saul who caused such havoc on the Church in Jerusalem that the Christians in that city scattered for their own safety.

It was Saul who took men and women of Christ, and put them in prison for their faith.

It was Saul who was so active and zealous in his persecution of the Saints that he was known and feared far beyond the confines of the city of Jerusalem.

It was Saul who vehemently continued to breathe out threats and slaughter against the disciples of the Lord

Surely, if ever there was a man who was an unlikely candidate for Christianity, it had to have been Saul.

Then one day on the road to Damascus, on a mission to further persecute the Christians, a brilliant and blinding light shone round about him, causing him to fall to the earth. He heard a voice say to him, "… Saul, Saul, why persecutest thou me?" (Acts 9:4).

Saul answered, "… Who art thou, Lord? …" (Acts 9:5).

"… I am Jesus whom thou persecutest…", the voice declared (Acts 9:5).

Trembling and astonished, Saul asked, "… Lord, what wilt thou have me to do?…" (Acts 9:6).

That question and the Lord's answer to it changed Saul forever. He changed by the grace of Christ from Saul, the persecutor of Christ, to Paul, the Apostle of Christ. It's interesting to me that he who consented to the death of the Christian martyr, Stephen, himself eventually died a Christian martyr.

If we call Jesus, Lord and Savior, do we have faith in His power to save us, and the ones we love?

Cornelius and Peter

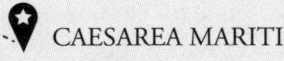 **CAESAREA MARITIMA** *Scriptures: Acts 10*

I sat in the ruins of the hippodrome in the ancient city of Caesarea, in modern-day Israel, looking out into the beautiful blue of the Mediterranean Sea as I listened to a gifted teacher, S. Michael Wilcox, relate a powerful story.

In that city, nearly 2,000 years ago, a man named Cornelius, a Roman centurion, experienced a vision from God. "Thy prayers and thine alms are come up for a memorial before God" (Acts 10:4) the angel said, and "...now send men to Joppa and call for one Simon, whose surname is Peter....He shall tell thee what thou oughtest to do" (Acts 10:5-6).

Cornelius responded immediately, and from Caesarea sent three of his most trusted men to Joppa to fetch Peter.

The next day about noon, Peter went up on the roof to pray. He became very hungry and asked for food. While they were preparing it, a vision was opened to Peter in which he saw a great sheet let down from heaven, full of all manner of beasts. A voice said to him, "Rise, Peter, kill and eat. But Peter said, not so, Lord; for I have never eaten anything that is common or unclean. And the voice spake unto him again the second time, What God hath cleansed, that call not thou common." This vision was repeated three times, and Peter had no idea what it meant.

Just then, the servants of Cornelius came to the door, and the Spirit whispered to Peter that he was to go with them for the Lord had sent them.

The next day at Caesarea, Peter walked in to meet Cornelius, and Cornelius fell down and worshiped him. "But Peter took him up, saying, Stand up; I myself also am a man" (Acts 10:25-26).

Peter then explained to the assembled crowd of gentiles that as a Jew it was unlawful for him to keep company with them, but as God had instructed, he was not to judge any man as common or unclean. "...I ask therefore," Peter said, "for what ye have sent for me?" (Acts 10:29).

Cornelius related his vision, and suddenly Peter understood his – that the world was about to change.

"...Of a truth," he said, "I perceive that God is no respecter of persons: But in every nation he that feareth him, and worketh righteousness, is accepted of him" (Acts 10:34-35).

To that point, the blessings of the gospel had been only for Abraham's children – the lost sheep of the House of Israel, but it was a new day and new age.

Peter then taught them of Jesus and the first principles of the restored Gospel of Christ, and while he spoke, the Holy Ghost fell upon them and they were converted and baptized – the first Christians not of Israel. That day changed the world forever.

As I sat there, it struck me in the heart with great power that it started here in the small coastal city of Caesarea in the tiny nation of Israel, and from here – right here – the gospel of Jesus Christ crossed the Mediterranean and went forth unto every nation, kindred, tongue, and people – until it reached the ears of this heathen, gentile boy of 18, in Idaho, 2000 years later.

This is my commandment, That ye love on another, as I have loved you.

John 15:12

About the Author
Glenn Rawson

Glenn Rawson has been telling stories for over 30 years. He started writing as a way to share his thoughts with family and a few close friends. An acquaintance who worked in radio asked him to record and share his stories with his audience. Listeners enjoyed hearing them, and the recordings quickly spread to dozens of other stations throughout the country.

Glenn has authored more than 20 books and written and produced over 100 TV documentaries. Over the years, he has connected with millions of people through print, radio and TV broadcasts, and online social media channels.

Glenn loves to research and write, but is happiest when he is traveling the world as a tour guide, sharing stories of history and the communities he visits with his guests. His goal is to help inspire and lift others with his stories.

For information about receiving weekly stories and other books available, please visit
GLENNRAWSONSTORIES.COM OR HISTORYOFTHESAINTS.ORG.

About the Artists
Kelsy and Jesse Lightweave

Kelsy and Jesse Lightweave have been creating powerful photographic illustrations as a wife-husband duo since 2013. Together, along with their 4 children, they've transformed their family hobby into a serious study and exploration of the Gospel of Jesus Christ through artistic portrayals. Their Immanuel pieces depict Christ's mission using symbols, color and contrasting luminance. The Savior is the emanating light that brings life to everything physical and spiritual--A light that is underscored by the necessary opposing darkness found in its absence. The hope for the saving light and its actualization in our lives is taught to us through the ministry of Jesus Christ. Each art piece they create tells a story and can teach the viewer about Christ's purpose and sacrifice for each one of us. Kelsy & Jesse shed a new perspective on the power of divine reflection, with the desire to share Christ's story and mission using a different kind of brush.

For information about Lightweave and to shop their artworks, visit their website:
www.lightweave.me